HOW
TO
PRAY

Of Other Worlds: Essays & Stories

Narrative Poems

Letters of C. S. Lewis

All My Road Before Me

The Business of Heaven: Daily Readings from C. S. Lewis

Present Concerns: Essays by C. S. Lewis

Spirits in Bondage: A Cycle of Lyrics

On Stories: And Other Essays of Literature

ALSO AVAILABLE FROM HARPERCOLLINS

The Chronicles of Narnia

The Magician's Nephew

The Lion, the Witch and the Wardrobe

The Horse and His Boy

Prince Caspian

The Voyage of the Dawn Treader

The Silver Chair

The Last Battle

HOW
TO
PRAY

REFLECTIONS AND ESSAYS

C. S. Lewis

HarperOne
An Imprint of HarperCollins*Publishers*

HarperOne

GOD IN THE DOCK. Copyright © 1967 by C. S. Lewis Pte. Ltd. Published by Eerdmans.

LETTERS TO AN AMERICAN LADY. Copyright © 1967 by C. S. Lewis Pte. Ltd. Published by Eerdmans.

HOW TO PRAY. Copyright © 2018 by C. S. Lewis Pte. Ltd. All rights reserved. Printed in the United States of America. No part of this book may be used or reproduced in any manner whatsoever without written permission except in the case of brief quotations embodied in critical articles and reviews. For information, address HarperCollins Publishers, 195 Broadway, New York, NY 10007.

Every effort has been made to obtain permissions for pieces quoted or adapted in this work. If any required acknowledgments have been omitted, or any rights overlooked, it is unintentional. Please notify the publishers of any omission, and it will be rectified in future editions.

HarperCollins books may be purchased for educational, business, or sales promotional use. For information, please email the Special Markets Department at SPsales@harpercollins.com.

FIRST EDITION

Designed by Yvonne Chan

Library of Congress Cataloging-in-Publication data is available upon request.

ISBN 978-0-06-284713-3

22 23 24   LSC   10 9 8 7 6 5 4

Master, they say that when I seem
To be in speech with you,
Since you make no replies, it's all a dream
—One talker aping two.
They are half right, but not as they
Imagine; rather, I
Seek in myself the things I meant to say,
And lo! the wells are dry.
Then, seeing me empty, you forsake
The Listener's role, and through
My dead lips breathe and into utterance wake
The thoughts I never knew.
And thus you neither need reply
Nor can; thus, while we seem
Two talking, thou art One forever, and I
No dreamer, but thy dream.

"PRAYER," *POEMS*

CONTENTS

Contents

Contents

PREFACE

C. S. LEWIS is widely recognized as one of the twentieth century's leading defenders and explainers of the Christian faith, especially through his classic works *Mere Christianity, The Screwtape Letters, Miracles, The Problem of Pain*, and more. What is ironic is that in private Lewis often expressed how his weakest moments were just after he had successfully defended a Christian idea or doctrine. What sustained him, though, was his commitment to living out what he saw as his ordinary Christian practices: attending church, practicing charity and hospitality, examining his motives and actions to lessen his weaknesses, confessing his sins, and strengthening what needed strengthening. And he prayed.

It is not surprising that a teacher of Christian faith would pray regularly, and it is easy to overlook the regular mentions of prayer in Lewis's many letters over the years. "I will keep you in my prayers" sounds like a cliché, even though phrases like this appear often and regularly in his correspondence. Taken as a whole, these many references reveal something important: that Lewis took his practice of prayer seriously. If we are paying attention, it soon becomes apparent that Lewis routinely committed to praying for people, that he kept lists of such requests, tracking and updating them over time, that he had his own list of requests, that he often prayed traditional prayers from the prayer book as well as practicing many other forms of prayers besides making petitions, and he regularly dispensed advice on issues surrounding prayer. In his published work, the subject of prayer pops up regularly. In other words, Lewis spent a lot of time practicing, thinking about, and writing about prayer.

It is also clear that Lewis saw all this as wholly unremarkable. In a brief letter of August 1949, Lewis said to a friend, "I don't feel I could write a book on Prayer: I think it would be rather 'cheek' of my part." He obviously changed his mind in that he began writing such a book, though it was only published posthumously as *Letters to Malcolm: Chiefly on Prayer*. But even here, the emphasis is explaining how to think about prayer more than providing a primer on praying (though some of that leaks through).

By publishing this new volume entitled *How to Pray*, we are making the argument that what Lewis saw as unremarkable is still remarkably important. By reading the pieces included here, it becomes clear that it was Lewis's long-term commitment to the practice of prayer that helps explain why his teachings have such depth and vibrancy even after many decades. Lewis never reduces the faith to mere intellectual or philosophical problems. Instead, his apologetic work was merely one dimension of what he experienced as a much larger reality, a reality grounded in a relationship with the living God. Even issues regarding prayer are presented within the larger frame of this relational foundation.

In *How to Pray*, we have tried to gather Lewis's wisdom on prayer sprinkled throughout his books, essays, letters, and poems—all of which appear within this volume. And because Lewis wrote as a lifelong practitioner of prayer, what he says is often wise, striking, and deep, which will not be a surprise to anyone who has looked to Lewis as a Christian guide and mentor before. For the sake of consistency and cohesion, we have retitled the pieces in the form of questions about prayer that the pieces could be said to answer. The pieces' original titles and sources are listed on the opening page of each chapter and at the end of the book. In each of the chapters, you will also find shorter excerpts on the topic as sidebars. We are indebted to and thankful for the thorough work of Zachary Kincaid, who researched and selected these pieces. Our hope in presenting this volume is that people will not only celebrate Lewis for what he said about Christianity but also for how he lived as a Christian. I hope by the end of the book you will say amen to that.

MICHAEL G. MAUDLIN
Senior vice president and executive editor
HarperOne

CAN PRAYER BE
PROVEN TO WORK?

SOME YEARS AGO I got up one morning intending to have my hair cut in preparation for a visit to London, and the first letter I opened made it clear I need not go to London. So I decided to put the haircut off too. But then there began the most unaccountable little nagging in my mind, almost like a voice saying, "Get it cut all the same. Go and get it cut." In the end I could stand it no longer. I went. Now my barber at that time was a fellow Christian and a man of many troubles whom my brother and I had sometimes been able to help. The moment I opened his shop door he

The World's Last Night (from "The Efficacy of Prayer").

said, "Oh, I was praying you might come today." And in fact if I had come a day or so later I should have been of no use to him.

It awed me; it awes me still. But of course one cannot rigorously prove a causal connection between the barber's prayers and my visit. It might be telepathy. It might be accident.

I have stood by the bedside of a woman whose thighbone was eaten through with cancer and who had thriving colonies of the disease in many other bones as well. It took three people to move her in bed. The doctors predicted a few months of life; the nurses (who often know better), a few weeks. A good man laid his hands on her and prayed. A year later the patient was walking (uphill, too, through rough woodland) and the man who took the last X-ray photos was saying, "These bones are as solid as rock. It's miraculous."

But once again there is no rigorous proof. Medicine, as all true doctors admit, is not an exact science. We need not invoke the supernatural to explain the falsification of its prophecies. You need not, unless you choose, believe in a causal connection between the prayers and the recovery.

The question then arises, "What sort of evidence would prove the efficacy of prayer?" The thing we pray for may happen, but how can you ever know it was not going to happen anyway? Even if the thing were indisputably miraculous it would not follow that the miracle had occurred because of your prayers. The answer surely is that a compulsive empirical proof such as we have in the sciences can never be attained.

Some things are proved by the unbroken uniformity of our experiences. The law of gravitation is established by the fact that, in our experience, all bodies without exception obey it. Now even if all the things that people prayed for happened, which they do not, this would not prove what Christians mean by the efficacy of prayer. For prayer is request. The essence of request, as distinct from compulsion, is that it may or may not be granted. And if an infinitely wise Being listens to the requests of finite and foolish creatures, of course He will sometimes grant and sometimes refuse them. Invariable "success" in prayer would not prove the Christian doctrine at all. It would prove something much more like magic—a power in certain human beings to control, or compel, the course of nature.

There are, no doubt, passages in the New Testament which may seem at first sight to promise an invariable granting of our prayers. But that cannot be what they really mean. For in the very heart of the story we meet a glaring instance to the contrary. In Gethsemane the holiest of all petitioners prayed three times that a certain cup might pass from Him. It did not. After that the idea that prayer is recommended to us as a sort of infallible gimmick may be dismissed.

Other things are proved not simply by experience but by those artificially contrived experiences which we call experiments. Could this be done about prayer? I will pass over the objection that no Christian could take part in such a project, because he has been forbid-

den it: "You must not try experiments on God, your
Master." Forbidden or not, is the thing even possible?

I have seen it suggested that a team of people—
the more the better—should agree to pray as hard as
they knew how, over a period of six weeks, for all the
patients in Hospital A and none of those in Hospital B. Then you would tot up the results and see if
A had more cures and fewer deaths. And I suppose
you would repeat the experiment at various times and
places so as to eliminate the influence of irrelevant
factors.

The trouble is that I do not see how any real prayer
could go on under such conditions. "Words without
thoughts never to heaven go," says the King in *Hamlet*. Simply to say prayers is not to pray; otherwise a
team of properly trained parrots would serve as well
as men for our experiment. You cannot pray for the
recovery of the sick unless the end you have in view
is their recovery. But you can have no motive for de-
siring the recovery of all the patients in one hospital
and none of those in another. You are not doing it in

order that suffering should be relieved; you are doing it to find out what happens. The real purpose and
the nominal purpose of your prayers are at variance.
In other words, whatever your tongue and teeth and
knees may do, you are not praying. The experiment
demands an impossibility.

Empirical proof and disproof are, then, unobtainable. But this conclusion will seem less depressing if
we remember that prayer is request and compare it
with other specimens of the same thing.

We make requests of our fellow creatures as well as
of God: we ask for the salt, we ask for a raise in pay,
we ask a friend to feed the cat while we are on our hol-
idays, we ask a woman to marry us. Sometimes we get
what we ask for and sometimes not. But when we do,
it is not nearly so easy as one might suppose to prove
with scientific certainty a causal connection between
the asking and the getting.

Your neighbour may be a humane person who
would not have let your cat starve even if you had
forgotten to make any arrangement. Your employer is

An ordinary simple Christian kneels down to say his prayers. He is trying to get into touch with God. But if he is a Christian he knows that what is prompting him to pray is also God: God, so to speak, inside him. But he also knows that all his real knowledge of God comes through Christ, the Man who was God—that Christ is standing beside him, helping him to pray, praying for him. You see what is happening. God is the thing to which he is praying—the goal he is trying to reach. God is also the thing inside him which is pushing him on—the motive power. God is also the road or bridge along which he is being pushed to that goal. So that the whole threefold life of the three-personal Being is actually going on in that ordinary little bedroom where an ordinary man is saying his prayers. The man is being caught up into the higher kinds of life—what I called *Zoe* or spiritual life: he is being pulled into God, by God, while still remaining himself.

—*MERE CHRISTIANITY*

never so likely to grant your request for a raise as when he is aware that you could get better money from a rival firm and is quite possibly intending to secure you by a raise in any case. As for the lady who consents to marry you—are you sure she had not decided to do so already? Your proposal, you know, might have been the result, not the cause, of her decision. A certain important conversation might never have taken place unless she had intended that it should.

Thus in some measure the same doubt that hangs about the causal efficacy of our prayers to God hangs also about our prayers to man. Whatever we get we might have been going to get anyway. But only, as I say, in some measure. Our friend, boss, and wife may tell us that they acted because we asked; and we may know them so well as to feel sure, first that they are saying what they believe to be true, and secondly that they understand their own motives well enough to be right. But notice that when this happens our assurance has not been gained by the methods of science. We do not try the control experiment of refusing the raise or breaking off the engagement and then making our request again under fresh conditions. Our assurance is quite different in kind from scientific knowledge. It is born out of our personal relation to the other parties; not from knowing things about them but from knowing *them*.

Our assurance—if we reach an assurance—that God always hears and sometimes grants our prayers, and that apparent grantings are not merely fortuitous, can only come in the same sort of way. There can be no question of tabulating successes and failures and trying to decide whether the successes are too numerous to be accounted for by chance. Those who best know a man best know whether, when he did what they asked, he did it because they asked. I think those who best know God will best know whether He sent me to the barber's shop because the barber prayed.

For up till now we have been tackling the whole question in the wrong way and on the wrong level. The very question "Does prayer work?" puts us in the wrong frame of mind from the outset. "Work": as if it were magic, or a machine—something that functions automatically. Prayer is either a sheer illusion or a personal contact between embryonic, incomplete persons (ourselves) and the utterly concrete Person. (Prayer in the sense of petition, asking for things, is a small part of it; confession and penitence are its threshold, adoration its sanctuary, the presence and vision and enjoyment of God its bread and wine.) In it God shows Himself to us. That He answers prayers is a corollary—not necessarily the most important one—from that revelation. What He does is learned from what He is.

Petitionary prayer is, nonetheless, both allowed and commanded to us: "Give us our daily bread." And no doubt it raises a theoretical problem. Can we believe that God ever really modifies His action in response to the suggestions of men? For infinite wisdom does not need telling what is best, and infinite goodness needs no urging to do it. But neither does God need any of those things that are done by finite agents, whether living or inanimate. He could, if He chose, repair our bodies miraculously without food; or give us food without the aid of farmers, bakers, and butchers; or knowledge without the aid of learned men; or convert the heathen without missionaries. Instead, He allows soils and weather and animals and the muscles, minds, and wills of men to co-operate in the execution of His will. "God," said Pascal, "instituted prayer in order to lend to His creatures the dignity of causality." But not only prayer; whenever we act at all He lends us that dignity. It is not really stranger, nor less strange, that my prayers should affect the course of events than that my other actions should do so. They have not advised or changed God's mind—that is, His overall purpose. But that purpose will be realized in different ways according to the actions, including the prayers, of His creatures.

For He seems to do nothing of Himself which He can possibly delegate to His creatures. He commands us to do slowly and blunderingly what He could do perfectly and in the twinkling of an eye. He allows us to neglect what He would have us do, or to fail. Perhaps we do not fully realize the problem, so to call it, of enabling finite free wills to co-exist with Omnipotence. It seems to involve at every moment almost a sort of divine abdication. We are not mere recipients or spectators. We are either privileged to share in the game or compelled to collaborate in the work, "to wield our little tridents." Is this amazing process simply Creation going on before our eyes? This is how (no light matter) God makes something—indeed, makes gods—out of nothing.

So at least it seems to me. But what I have offered can be, at the very best, only a mental model or symbol. All that we say on such subjects must be merely analogical and parabolic. The reality is doubtless not comprehensible by our faculties. But we can at any rate try to expel bad analogies and bad parables. Prayer is not a machine. It is not magic. It is not advice offered to God. Our act, when we pray, must not, any more than all our other acts, be separated from the continuous act of God Himself, in which alone all finite causes operate.

"Praying for particular things," said I, "always seems to me like advising God how to run the world. Wouldn't it be wiser to assume that He knows best?" "On the same principle," said he, "I suppose you never ask a man next to you to pass the salt, because God knows best whether you ought to have salt or not. And I suppose you never take an umbrella, because God knows best whether you ought to be wet or dry." "That's quite different," I protested. "I don't see why," said he. "The odd thing is that He should let us influence the course of events at all. But since He lets us do it in one way, I don't see why He shouldn't let us do it in the other."

—"SCRAPS," *GOD IN THE DOCK*

It would be even worse to think of those who get what they pray for as a sort of court favorites, people who have influence with the throne. The refused prayer of Christ in Gethsemane is answer enough to that. And I dare not leave out the hard saying which

I once heard from an experienced Christian: "I have seen many striking answers to prayer and more than one that I thought miraculous. But they usually come at the beginning: before conversion, or soon after it. As the Christian life proceeds, they tend to be rarer. The refusals, too, are not only more frequent; they become more unmistakable, more emphatic."

Does God then forsake just those who serve Him best? Well, He who served Him best of all said, near His tortured death, "Why hast thou forsaken me?" When God becomes man, that Man, of all others, is least comforted by God, at His greatest need. There is a mystery here which, even if I had the power, I might not have the courage to explore. Meanwhile, little people like you and me, if our prayers are sometimes granted, beyond all hope and probability, had better not draw hasty conclusions to our own advantage. If we were stronger, we might be less tenderly treated. If we were braver, we might be sent, with far less help, to defend far more desperate posts in the great battle.

꒰

WHY MAKE REQUESTS
OF GOD IF HE ALREADY
KNOWS WHAT WE NEED?

"EVEN IF I grant your point and admit that answers to prayer are theoretically possible, I shall still
think they are infinitely improbable. I don't think it
at all likely that God requires the ill-informed (and
contradictory) advice of us humans as to how to run
the world. If He is all-wise, as you say He is, doesn't
He know already what is best? And if He is all-good,
won't He do it whether we pray or not?"

This is the case against prayer which has, in the last
hundred years, intimidated thousands of people. The

God in the Dock (from the chapter titled "Work and Prayer").

usual answer is that it applies only to the lowest sort of prayer, the sort that consists in asking for things to happen. The higher sort, we are told, offers no advice to God; it consists only of "communion" or intercourse with Him; and those who take this line seem to suggest that the lower kind of prayer really is an absurdity and that only children or savages would use it.

I have never been satisfied with this view. The distinction between the two sorts of prayer is a sound one; and I think on the whole (I am not quite certain) that the sort which asks for nothing is the higher or more advanced. To be in the state in which you are so at one with the will of God that you wouldn't want to alter the course of events even if you could is certainly a very high or advanced condition.

But if one simply rules out the lower kind two difficulties follow. In the first place, one has to say that the whole historical tradition of Christian prayer (including the Lord's Prayer itself) has been wrong: for it has always admitted prayers for our daily bread, for the recovery of the sick, for protection from enemies, for the conversion of the outside world and the like. In the second place, though the other kind of prayer may be "higher" if you restrict yourself to it because you have got beyond the desire to use any other, there is nothing specially "high" or "spiritual" about abstaining from prayers that make requests simply because you think they're no good. It might be a very pretty thing (but, again, I'm not absolutely certain) if a little boy never asked for cake because he was so high-minded and spiritual that he didn't want any cake. But there's nothing specially pretty about a little boy who doesn't ask because he has learned that it is no use asking. I think that the whole matter needs reconsideration.

The case against prayer (I mean the "low" or old-fashioned kind) is this. The thing you ask for is either good—for you and for the world in general—or else it is not. If it is, then a good and wise God will do it anyway. If it is not, then He won't. In neither case can your prayer make any difference. But if this argument is sound, surely it is an argument not only against praying, but against doing anything whatever?

In every action, just as in every prayer, you are trying to bring about a certain result; and this result must be good or bad. Why, then, do we not argue as the opponents of prayer argue, and say that if the intended result is good God will bring it to pass without your interference, and that if it is bad He will prevent it happening whatever you do? Why wash your hands? If God intends them to be clean, they'll come clean without your washing them. If He doesn't, they'll remain dirty (as Lady Macbeth found) however much soap you use. Why ask for the salt? Why put on your boots? Why do anything?

We know that we can act and that our actions produce results. Everyone who believes in God must therefore admit (quite apart from the question of prayer) that God has not chosen to write the whole of history with His own hand. Most of the events that go on in the universe are indeed out of our control, but not all. It is like a play in which the scene and the general outline of the story is fixed by the author, but certain minor details are left for the actors to improvise. It may be a mystery why He should have allowed us to cause real events at all; but it is no odder that He should allow us to cause them by praying than by any other method.

ↄ

Don't bother about the idea that God "has known for millions of years exactly what you are about to pray". That isn't what it's like. God is hearing you *now*, just as simply as a mother hears a child. The difference His timelessness makes is that this *now* (which slips away from you even as you say the word *now*) is for Him infinite. If you must think of His timelessness at all, don't think of Him *having* looked forward to this moment for millions of years: think that to Him you are always praying this prayer. But there's really no need to bring it in. You have gone into the Temple ("one day in Thy court is better than a thousand") and found Him, as always, there. That is all you need to bother about.

—*COLLECTED LETTERS*, AUGUST 1, 1949,
TO MISS BRECKENRIDGE

Pascal says that God "instituted prayer in order to allow His creatures the dignity of causality". It would perhaps be truer to say that He invented both prayer and physical action for that purpose. He gave us small creatures the dignity of being able to contribute to the course of events in two different ways. He made the matter of the universe such that we can (in those limits) do things to it; that is why we can wash our own hands and feed or murder our fellow creatures. Similarly, He made His own plan or plot of history such that it admits a certain amount of free play and can be modified in response to our prayers. If it is foolish and impudent to ask for victory in a war (on the grounds that God might be expected to know best), it would be equally foolish and impudent to put on a mackintosh—does not God know best whether you ought to be wet or dry?

The two methods by which we are allowed to produce events may be called work and prayer. Both are alike in this respect—that in both we try to produce a state of affairs which God has not (or at any rate not yet) seen fit to provide "on His own". And from this point of view the old maxim *laborare est orare* (work is prayer) takes on a new meaning. What we do when we weed a field is not quite different from what we do when we pray for a good harvest. But there is an important difference all the same.

You cannot be sure of a good harvest whatever you do to a field. But you can be sure that if you pull up one weed that one weed will no longer be there. You can be sure that if you drink more than a certain amount of alcohol you will ruin your health or that if you go on for a few centuries more wasting the resources of the planet on wars and luxuries you will shorten the life of the whole human race. The kind of causality we exercise by work is, so to speak, divinely guaranteed, and therefore ruthless. By it we are free to do ourselves as much harm as we please. But the kind which we exercise by prayer is not like that; God has left Himself a discretionary power. Had He not done so, prayer would be an activity too dangerous for man and we should have the horrible state of things envisaged by Juvenal: "Enormous prayers which Heaven in anger grants" (*Satires*, Book IV, Satire x, line 111).

Prayers are not always—in the crude, factual sense of the word—"granted". This is not because prayer is a weaker kind of causality, but because it is a stronger kind. When it "works" at all it works unlimited by space and time. That is why God has retained a discretionary power of granting or refusing it; except on that condition prayer would destroy us. It is not unreasonable for a headmaster to say, "Such and such things you may do according to the fixed rules of this school. But such and such other things are too dangerous to be left to general rules. If you want to do them you must come and make a request and talk over the whole matter with me in my study. And then— we'll see."

DO OUR PRAYERS DEPEND ON HOW DEEPLY WE FEEL OR MEAN THEM?

ONE REASON WHY the Enemy found this so easy was that, without knowing it, I was already desperately anxious to get rid of my religion; and that for a reason worth recording. By a sheer mistake—and I still believe it to have been an honest mistake—in spiritual technique I had rendered my private practice of that religion a quite intolerable burden. It came about in this way. Like everyone else I had been told as a child that one must not only say one's prayers but think about what one was saying. Accordingly,

---

Surprised by Joy (from chapter 4, "I Broaden My Mind").

when (at Oldie's) I came to a serious belief, I tried to put this into practice. At first it seemed plain sailing. But soon the false conscience (St Paul's 'Law', Herbert's 'prattler') came into play. One had no sooner reached 'Amen' than it whispered, 'Yes. But are you sure you were really thinking about what you said?'; then, more subtly, 'Were you, for example, thinking about it as well as you did last night?' The answer, for reasons I did not then understand, was nearly always No. 'Very well,' said the voice, 'hadn't you, then, better try it over again?' And one obeyed; but of course with no assurance that the second attempt would be any better.

To these nagging suggestions my reaction was, on the whole, the most foolish I could have adopted. I set myself a standard. No clause of my prayer was to be allowed to pass muster unless it was accompanied by what I called a 'realisation', by which I meant a certain vividness of the imagination and the affections. My nightly task was to produce by sheer willpower a phenomenon which willpower could never produce, which was so ill-defined that I could never say with absolute confidence whether it had occurred, and which, even when it did occur, was of very mediocre spiritual value. If only someone had read to me old Walter Hilton's warning that we must never in prayer strive to extort 'by maistry' what God does not give! But no one did; and night after night, dizzy with desire for sleep and often in a kind of despair, I endeavoured to pump up my 'realisations'. The thing threatened to become an infinite regress. One began of course by praying for good 'realisations'. But had that pre-liminary prayer itself been 'realised'? This question I think I still had enough sense to dismiss; otherwise it might have been as difficult to begin my prayers as to end them. How it all comes back! The cold oil-cloth, the quarters chiming, the night slipping past, the sick-ening, hopeless weariness. This was the burden from which I longed with soul and body to escape. It had already brought me to such a pass that the nightly tor-ment projected its gloom over the whole evening, and I dreaded bedtime as if I were a chronic sufferer from

❧

"Whether it is any good praying for actual things"—the first question is what one means by "any good". Is it a good thing to do? Yes: however we explain it, we are told to ask for particular things such as our daily bread. Does it "work"? Certainly not like a mechanical operation or a magical spell. It is a request which of course the Other Party may or may not, for His own good reasons, grant. But how can it change God's will? Well—but how v. odd it would be if God in His actions towards me were bound to ignore what I did (including my prayers). Surely He hasn't to forgive me for sins I didn't commit or to cure me of errors into which I have never fallen? In other words His will (however changeless in some ultimate metaphysical sense) must be related to what I am and do. And once grant that, and why should my asking or not asking not be one of the things He takes into account? At any rate He said He would—and He ought to know. (We often talk as if He were not very good at Theology!)

> I certainly believe (now really, long since with a merely intellectual assent) that a sin once repented and forgiven, is gone, annihilated, burnt up in the fire of Divine Love, white as snow. There is no harm in continuing to "bewail" it, i.e., to express one's sorrow, but not to ask for pardon, for that you already have—one's sorrow for being that sort of person. Your conscience need not be "burdened" with it in the sense of feeling that you have an unsettled account, but you can still in a sense be patiently and (in a sense) contentedly humbled by it....
>
> —*COLLECTED LETTERS*, JANUARY 8, 1952,
> TO MRS. LOCKLEY

insomnia. Had I pursued the same road much further I think I should have gone mad.

This ludicrous burden of false duties in prayer provided, of course, an unconscious motive for wishing to shuffle off the Christian faith; but about the same time, or a little later, conscious causes of doubt arose. One came from reading the classics. Here, especially in Virgil, one was presented with a mass of religious ideas; and all teachers and editors took it for granted from the outset that these religious ideas were sheer illusion. No one ever attempted to show in what sense Christianity fulfilled Paganism or Paganism prefigured Christianity. The accepted position seemed to be that religions were normally a mere farrago of nonsense, though our own, by a fortunate exception, was exactly true. The other religions were not even explained, in the earlier Christian fashion, as the work of devils. That I might, conceivably, have been brought to believe. But the impression I got was that religion in general, though utterly false, was a natural growth, a kind of endemic nonsense into which humanity tended to blunder. In the midst of a thousand such religions stood our own, the thousand and first, labelled True. But on what grounds could I believe in this exception? It obviously was in some general sense the same kind of thing as all the rest. Why was it so differently treated? Need I, at any rate, continue to treat it differently? I was very anxious not to.

In addition to this, and equally working against my faith, there was in me a deeply ingrained pessimism; a pessimism, by that time, much more of intellect than of temper. I was now by no means unhappy; but I had very definitely formed the opinion that the universe was, in the main, a rather regrettable institution. I am well aware that some will feel disgust and some will laugh, at the idea of a loutish, well-fed boy in an Eton collar, passing an unfavourable judgement on the cosmos. They may be right in either reaction, but no more right because I wore an Eton collar. They are forgetting what boyhood felt like from within. Dates are not so important as people believe. I fancy that most of

"Our morning prayer should be that in the Imitation: *Da hodie perfecte incipere*—grant me to make an unflawed beginning today, for I have done nothing yet."

—"A SLIP OF THE TONGUE," *THE WEIGHT OF GLORY*

those who think at all have done a great deal of thinking in the first fourteen years. As to the sources of my
pessimism, the reader will remember that though in
many ways most fortunate, yet I had very early in life
met a great dismay. But I am now inclined to think
that the seeds of pessimism were sown before my
mother's death. Ridiculous as it may sound, I believe
that the clumsiness of my hands was at the root of the
matter. How could this be? Not, certainly, that a child
says, 'I can't cut a straight line with a pair of scissors,
therefore the universe is evil.' Childhood has no such
power of generalisation and is not (to do it justice)
so silly. Nor did my clumsiness produce what is ordinarily called an Inferiority Complex. I was not comparing myself with other boys; my defeats occurred
in solitude. What they really bred in me was a deep
(and, of course, inarticulate) sense of resistance or
opposition on the part of inanimate things. Even that
makes it too abstract and adult. Perhaps I had better
call it a settled expectation that everything would do
what you did not want it to do. Whatever you wanted

to remain straight, would bend; whatever you tried to bend would fly back to the straight; all knots which you wished to be firm would come untied; all knots you wanted to untie would remain firm. It is not possible to put it into language without making it comic, and I have indeed no wish to see it (now) except as something comic. But it is perhaps just these early experiences which are so fugitive and, to an adult, so grotesque, that give the mind its earliest bias, its habitual sense of what is or is not plausible.

ISN'T IT PRESUMPTUOUS FOR US TO BRING OUR CONCERNS BEFORE GOD?

I PRESUME THAT only God's attention keeps me (or anything else) in existence at all.

What, then, are we really doing? Our whole conception of, so to call it, the prayer-situation depends on the answer.

We are always completely, and therefore equally, known to God. That is our destiny whether we like it or not. But though this knowledge never varies, the quality of our being known can. A school of thought holds that "freedom is willed necessity". Never mind

---

Letters to Malcolm (from chapter 4).

if they are right or not. I want this idea only as an analogy. Ordinarily, to be known by God is to be, for this purpose, in the category of things. We are, like earthworms, cabbages, and nebulae, objects of Divine knowledge. But when we (a) become aware of the fact—the present fact, not the generalisation—and (b) assent with all our will to be so known, then we treat ourselves, in relation to God, not as things but as persons. We have unveiled. Not that any veil could have baffled His sight. The change is in us. The passive changes to the active. Instead of merely being known, we show, we tell, we offer ourselves to view.

To put ourselves thus on a personal footing with God could, in itself and without warrant, be nothing but presumption and illusion. But we are taught that it is not; that it is God who gives us that footing. For it is by the Holy Spirit that we cry "Father". By unveiling, by confessing our sins and "making known" our requests, we assume the high rank of persons before Him. And He, descending, becomes a Person to us.

But I should not have said "becomes". In Him there is no becoming. He reveals Himself as Person: or reveals that in Him which is Person. For—dare one say it? in a book it would need pages of qualification and insurance—God is in some measure to a man as that man is to God. The door in God that opens is the door he knocks at. (At least, I think so, usually.) The Person in Him—He is more than a person—meets those who can welcome or at least face it. He speaks as "I" when we truly call Him "Thou". (How good Buber is!)

This talk of "meeting" is, no doubt, anthropomorphic; as if God and I could be face to face, like two fellow-creatures, when in reality He is above me and within me and below me and all about me. That is why it must be balanced by all manner of metaphysical and theological abstractions. But never, here or anywhere else, let us think that while anthropomorphic images are a concession to our weakness, the abstractions are the literal truth. Both are equally concessions; each singly misleading, and the two together mutually

Incidentally, since I have begun to pray, I find my extreme view of personality changing. My own empirical self is becoming more important and this is exactly the opposite of self love. You don't teach a seed how to die into treehood by throwing it into the fire: and it has to become a good seed before it's worth burying.

—*COLLECTED LETTERS*, DECEMBER 1935,
TO OWEN BARFIELD

corrective. Unless you sit to it very lightly, continually murmuring "Not thus, not thus, neither is this Thou", the abstraction is fatal. It will make the life of lives inanimate and the love of loves impersonal. The naïf image is mischievous chiefly in so far as it holds unbelievers back from conversion. It does believers, even at its crudest, no harm. What soul ever perished for believing that God the Father really has a beard?

Your other question is one which, I think, really gets in pious people's way. It was, you remember,

"How important must a need or desire be before we can properly make it the subject of a petition?" *Properly*, I take it, here means either "Without irreverence" or "Without silliness", or both.

When I'd thought about it for a bit, it seemed to me that there are really two questions involved.

(1) How important must an object be before we can, without sin and folly, allow our desire for it to become a matter of serious concern to us? This, you see, is a question about what old writers call our "frame"; that is, our "frame of mind".

(2) Granted the existence of such a serious concern in our minds, can it always be properly laid before God in prayer?

We all know the answer to the first of these in theory. We must aim at what St. Augustine (is it?) calls "ordinate loves". Our deepest concern should be for first things, and our next deepest for second things, and so on down to zero—to total absence of concern for things that are not really good, nor means to good, at all.

Meantime, however, we want to know not how we should pray if we were perfect but how we should pray being as we now are. And if my idea of prayer as "unveiling" is accepted, we have already answered this. It is no use to ask God with factitious earnestness for A when our whole mind is in reality filled with the desire for B. We must lay before Him what is in us, not what ought to be in us.

Even an intimate human friend is ill-used if we talk to him about one thing while our mind is really on another, and even a human friend will soon become aware when we are doing so. You yourself came to see me a few years ago when the great blow had fallen upon me. I tried to talk to you as if nothing were wrong. You saw through it in five minutes. Then I confessed. And you said things which made me ashamed of my attempt at concealment.

It may well be that the desire can be laid before God only as a sin to be repented; but one of the best ways of learning this is to lay it before God. Your problem, however, was not about sinful desires in

that sense; rather about desires, intrinsically innocent and sinning, if at all, only by being stronger
than the triviality of their object warrants. I have
no doubt at all that if they are the subject of our
thoughts they must be the subject of our prayers—
whether in penitence or in petition or in a little of
both: penitence for the excess, yet petition for the
thing we desire.

If one forcibly excludes them, don't they wreck all
the rest of our prayers? If we lay all the cards on the
table, God will help us to moderate the excesses. But
the pressure of things we are trying to keep out of
our mind is a hopeless distraction. As someone said,
"No noise is so emphatic as one you are trying not to
listen to."

The ordinate frame of mind is one of the blessings
we must pray for, not a fancy-dress we must put on
when we pray.

And perhaps, as those who do not turn to God in
petty trials will have no *habit* or such resort to help
them when the great trials come, so those who have

not learned to ask Him for childish things will have less readiness to ask Him for great ones. We must not be too high-minded. I fancy we may sometimes be deterred from small prayers by a sense of our own dignity rather than of God's.

HOW DOES PRAYER FIT WITH THE IDEA OF GOD'S PROVIDENCE? ARE WE ASKING FOR MIRACLES WHEN WE PRAY?

[THERE ARE] TWO classes of events and two only—miracles and natural events. The former are not interlocked with the history of Nature in the backward direction—i.e., in the time before their occurrence. The latter are. Many pious people, however, speak of certain events as being 'providential' or 'special providences' without meaning that they are miraculous. This generally implies a belief that, quite

---

Miracles (from Appendix B: "On 'Special Providences'").

apart from miracles, some events are providential in a sense in which some others are not. Thus some people thought that the weather which enabled us to bring off so much of our army at Dunkirk was 'providential' in some way in which weather as a whole is not providential. The Christian doctrine that some events, though not miracles, are yet answers to prayer, would seem at first to imply this.

I find it very difficult to conceive an intermediate class of events which are neither miraculous nor merely 'ordinary'. Either the weather at Dunkirk was or was not that which the previous physical history of the universe, by its own character, would inevitably produce. If it was, then how is it 'specially' providential? If it was not, then it was a miracle.

It seems to me, therefore, that we must abandon the idea that there is any special class of events (apart from miracles) which can be distinguished as 'specially providential'. Unless we are to abandon the conception of Providence altogether, and with it the belief in efficacious prayer, it follows that all events are equally providential. If God directs the course of events at all then he directs the movement of every atom at every moment; 'not one sparrow falls to the ground' without that direction. The 'naturalness' of natural events does not consist in being somehow outside God's providence. It consists in their being interlocked with one another inside a common space-time in accordance with the fixed pattern of the 'laws'.

In order to get any picture at all of a thing, it is sometimes necessary to begin with a false picture and then correct it. The false picture of Providence (false because it represents God and Nature as being both contained in a common Time) would be as follows. Every event in Nature results from some previous event, not from the laws of Nature. In the long run the first natural event, whatever it was, has dictated every other event. That is, when God at the moment of creation fed the first event into the framework of the 'laws'—first set the ball rolling—He determined the whole history of Nature. Foreseeing every part of that history, He intended every part of it. If He had wished for different weather at Dunkirk, He would have made the first event slightly different.

The weather we actually had is therefore in the strictest sense providential; it was decreed, and decreed for a purpose, when the world was made—but no more so (though more interestingly to us) than the precise position at this moment of every atom in the ring of Saturn.

It follows (still retaining our false picture) that every physical event was determined so as to serve a great number of purposes.

Thus God must be supposed in predetermining the weather at Dunkirk to have taken fully into account the effect it would have not only on the destiny of two nations but (what is incomparably more important) on all the individuals involved on both sides, on all animals, vegetables and minerals within range, and finally on every atom in the universe. This may sound excessive, but in reality we are attributing to the Omniscient only an infinitely superior degree of the same kind of skill which a mere human novelist exercises daily in constructing his plot.

Suppose I am writing a novel. I have the following problems on my hands: (1) Old Mr A. has got to be dead before Chapter 15. (2) And he'd better die suddenly because I have to prevent him from altering his will. (3) His daughter (my heroine) has got to be kept out of London for three chapters at least. (4) My hero has somehow got to recover the heroine's good opinion which he lost in Chapter 7. (5) That young prig B. who has to improve before the end of the book, needs a bad moral shock to take the conceit out of him. (6) We haven't decided on B.'s job yet; but the whole development of his character will involve giving him a job and showing him actually at work. How on earth am I to get in all these six things? . . . I have it. What about a railway accident? Old A. can be killed in it, and that settles him. In fact the accident can occur while he is actually going up to London to see his solicitor with the very purpose of getting his will altered. What more natural than that his daughter should run up with him? We'll have her slightly injured in the accident: that'll prevent her reaching London for as many chapters as we need. And the hero can be on the same train. He can behave with great coolness and heroism during the accident—probably he'll rescue the heroine from a burning carriage. That settles my fourth point. And the young prig B.? We'll make him the signalman whose negligence caused the accident. That gives him his moral shock and also links him up with the main plot. In fact, once we have thought of the railway accident, that single event will solve six apparently separate problems.

No doubt this is in some ways an intolerably misleading image: firstly because (except as regards the prig B.) I have been thinking not of the ultimate good of my characters but of the entertainment of my readers: secondly because we are simply ignoring the effect of the railway accident on all the other passengers in that train: and finally because it is I who make B. give the wrong signal. That is, though I pretend that he has free will, he really hasn't. In spite of these objections, however, the example may perhaps suggest how Divine ingenuity could so contrive the physical 'plot' of the universe as to provide a 'providential' answer to the needs of innumerable creatures.

But some of these creatures have free will. It is at this point that we must begin to correct the admittedly false picture of Providence which we have hitherto been using. That picture, you will remember, was false because it represented God and Nature as inhabiting a common Time. But it is probable that Nature is not really in Time and almost certain that God is not. Time is probably (like perspective) the mode of our perception. There is therefore in reality no question of God's at one point in time (the moment of creation) adapting the material history of the universe in advance to free acts which you or I are to perform at a later point in Time. To Him all the physical events and all the human acts are present in an eternal Now. The liberation of finite wills and the creation of the whole material history of the universe (related to the acts of those wills in all the necessary complexity)

Whether any individual Christian who attempts Faith Healing is prompted by genuine faith and charity or by spiritual pride is I take it a question we cannot decide. That is between God and him. Whether the cure occurs in any given case is clearly a question for the doctors. I am speaking now of healing by some *act* such as anointing or laying on of hands. *Praying* for the sick, i.e., praying simply, without any overt act, is unquestionably right and indeed we are commanded to pray for all men. And *of course* your prayers can do real good. Needless to say they don't do it either as a medicine does or as magic is supposed to do, i.e., automatically. Prayer is a request.... One cannot establish the efficacy of prayer by statistics.... It remains a matter of faith and of God's personal action; it would become a matter of demonstration only if it were impersonal or mechanical. When I say "personal" I do not mean private or individual. All our prayers are united with Christ's perpetual prayer and are part of the Church's prayer.

(In praying for people one dislikes I find it help-
ful to remember that one is joining in *His* prayer
for them.)

—*COLLECTED LETTERS*, JANUARY 5, 1951,
TO MRS. ARNOLD

is to Him a single operation. In this sense God did
not create the universe long ago but creates it at this
minute—at every minute.

Suppose I find a piece of paper on which a black
wavy line is already drawn, I can now sit down and
draw other lines (say in red) so shaped as to combine
with the black line into a pattern. Let us now suppose
that the original black line is conscious. But it is not
conscious along the whole length at once—only on
each point on that length in turn.

Its consciousness in fact is travelling along that line
from left to right retaining point A only as a memory
when it reaches B and unable until it has left B to become conscious of C. Let us also give this black line

free will. It chooses the direction it goes in. The particular wavy shape of it is the shape it wills to have. But whereas it is aware of its own chosen shape only moment by moment and does not know at point D which way it will decide to turn at point F, I can see its shape as a whole and all at once. At every moment it will find my red lines waiting for it and adapted to it. Of course: because I, in composing the total red-and-black design have the whole course of the black line in view and take it into account. It is a matter not of impossibility but merely of designer's skill for me to devise red lines which at every point have a right relation not only to the black line but to one another so as to fill the whole paper with a satisfactory design.

In this model the black line represents a creature with free will, the red lines represent material events, and I represent God. The model would of course be more accurate if I were making the paper as well as the pattern and if there were hundreds of millions of black lines instead of one—but for the sake of simplicity we must keep it as it is.

It will be seen that if the black line addressed prayers to me I might (if I chose) grant them. It prays that when it reaches point N it may find the red lines arranged around it in a certain shape. That shape may by the laws of design require to be balanced by other arrangements of red lines on quite different parts of the paper—some at the top or bottom so far away from the black line that it knows nothing about them: some so far to the left that they come before the beginning of the black line, some so far to the right that they come after its end. (The black line would call these parts of the paper, 'The time before I was born,' and, 'The time after I'm dead.') But these other parts of the pattern demanded by that red shape which Black Line wants at N, do not prevent my granting its prayer. For his whole course has been visible to me from the moment I looked at the paper and his requirements at point N are among the things I took into account in deciding the total pattern.

Most of our prayers if fully analysed, ask either for a miracle or for events whose foundation will have to have been laid before I was born, indeed, laid when the universe began. But then to God (though not to me) I and the prayer I make in 1945 were just as much present at the creation of the world as they are now and will be a million years hence. God's creative act is timeless and timelessly adapted to the 'free' elements within it: but this timeless adaptation meets our consciousness as a sequence and prayer and answer.

Two corollaries follow:

1. People often ask whether a given event (not a miracle) was really an answer to prayer or not. I think that if they analyse their thought they will find they are asking, 'Did God bring it about for a special purpose or would it have happened anyway as part of the natural course of events?' But this (like the old question, 'Have you left off beating your wife?') makes either answer impossible. In the play, *Hamlet*, Ophelia climbs out on a branch overhanging a river: the branch breaks, she falls in and drowns. What would you reply if anyone asked, 'Did Ophelia die because Shakespeare for poetic reasons wanted her to die at

that moment—or because the branch broke?' I think one would have to say, 'For both reasons.' Every event in the play happens as a result of other events in the play, but also every event happens because the poet wants it to happen. All events in the play are Shakespearian events; similarly all events in the real world are providential events. All events in the play, however, come about (or ought to come about) by the dramatic logic of events. Similarly all events in the real world (except miracles) come about by natural causes. 'Providence' and Natural causation are not alternatives; both determine every event because both are one.

2. When we are praying about the result, say, of a battle or a medical consultation, the thought will often cross our minds that (if only we knew it) the event is already decided one way or the other. I believe this to be no good reason for ceasing our prayers. The event certainly has been decided—in a sense it was decided 'before all worlds'. But one of the things taken into account in deciding it, and therefore one of

the things that really cause it to happen, may be this very prayer that we are now offering. Thus, shocking as it may sound, I conclude that we can at noon become part causes of an event occurring at ten a.m. (Some scientists would find this easier than popular thought does.) The imagination will, no doubt, try to play all sorts of tricks on us at this point. It will ask, 'Then if I stop praying can God go back and alter what has already happened?' No. The event has already happened and one of its causes has been the fact that you are asking such questions instead of praying. It will ask, 'Then if I begin to pray can God go back and alter what has already happened?' No. The event has already happened and one of its causes is your present prayer. Thus something does really depend on my choice. My free act contributes to the cosmic shape. That contribution is made in eternity or 'before all worlds'; but my consciousness of contributing reaches me at a particular point in the time-series.

The following question may be asked: If we can reasonably pray for an event which must in fact have happened or failed to happen several hours ago, why can we not pray for an event which we know *not* to have happened?, e.g., pray for the safety of someone who, as we know, was killed yesterday. What makes the difference is precisely our knowledge. The known event states God's will. It is psychologically impossible to pray for what we know to be unobtainable; and if it were possible the prayer would sin against the duty of submission to God's known will.

One more consequence remains to be drawn. It is never possible to prove empirically that a given, non-miraculous event was or was not an answer to prayer. Since it was non-miraculous the sceptic can always point to its natural causes and say, 'Because of these it would have happened anyway,' and the believer can always reply, 'But because these were only links in a chain of events, hanging on other links, and the whole chain hanging upon God's will, they may have occurred because someone prayed.' The efficacy of prayer, therefore, cannot be either asserted or denied without an exercise of the will—the will choosing or rejecting faith in the light of a whole philosophy. Experimental evidence there can be none on either side. In the sequence M.N.O. event N, unless it is a miracle, is always caused by M and causes O; but the real question is whether the total series (say A–Z) does or does not originate in a will that can take human prayers into account.

This impossibility of empirical proof is a spiritual necessity. A man who knew empirically that an event had been caused by his prayer would feel like a magician. His head would turn and his heart would be corrupted. The Christian is not to ask whether this or that event happened because of a prayer. He is rather to believe that all events without exception are *answers* to prayer in the sense that whether they are grantings or refusals the prayers of all concerned and their needs have all been taken into account. All prayers are heard, though not all prayers are granted. We must not picture destiny as a film unrolling for the most part on its own, but in which our prayers are sometimes allowed to insert additional items. On the contrary; what the film displays to us as it unrolls already contains the results of our prayers and of all our other acts. There is no question *whether* an event has happened because of your prayer. When the event you prayed for occurs, your prayer has always contributed to it. When the opposite event occurs, your prayer has never been ignored; it has been considered and refused, for your ultimate good and the good of the whole universe. (For example, because it is better for you and for everyone else in the long run that other people, including wicked ones, should exercise free will than that you should be protected from cruelty or treachery by turning the human race into automata.) But this is, and must remain, a matter of faith. You will, I think, only deceive yourself by trying to find special evidence for it in some cases more than in others.

DOES PRAYER REQUIRE
MORBID INTROSPECTION
OF OUR SINS?

WHEN GOD LOOKS into your office, or parish, or school, or hospital, or factory, or home, He sees all these people like that, and of course, sees one more, the one whom you do not see. For we may be quite certain that, just as in other people, there is something on which our best endeavors have again and again been shipwrecked, so in us there is something quite equally fatal, on which their endeavors have again and again been shipwrecked. If we are beginners in the Christian life, we have nothing to make the fatal

---

God in the Dock (from the chapter titled "Miserable Offenders").

flaw clear to ourselves. Does the person with a smelly breath know it smells? Or does the Club bore know he is a bore? Is there a single man or woman who believes himself or herself to be a bore or temperamentally jealous? Yet the world is pretty well sprinkled with bores and jealous people. If we are like that, everyone else will know it before we do. You ask why your friends have not told you about it. But what if they have? They may have tried again and again; but on every occasion, we thought they were being queer, that they were in a bad temper, or simply mistaken. They have tried again and again, and have probably now given it up.

What should be done about it? What is the good of my talking about the fatal flaw if one does not know about it? I think the first step is to get down to the flaws which one does know. I am speaking to Christians. Many of you, no doubt, are very far ahead of me in the Christian way. It is not for me to decide whether you should confess your sins to a priest or not (our Prayer Book leaves that free to all and de-

I think you are perfectly right to change your manner of prayer from time to time and I should suppose that all who pray seriously do thus change it. One's needs and capacities change and also, for creatures like us, excellent prayers may "go dead" if we use them too long. Whether one shd use written prayers composed by other people, or one's own words, or wordless prayer, or in what proportion one should mix all three, seems entirely a question for each individual to answer from his own experience. I myself find prayers without words the best *when* I can manage it, but can do so only when least distracted and in the best spiritual and bodily health (or what I think best). But another person might find it quite otherwise.

—*COLLECTED LETTERS*, OCTOBER 20, 1952,
TO MRS. ARNOLD

mands it of none) but if you do not, you should at least make a list on a piece of paper, and make a serious act of penance about each one of them. There is something about the mere words, you know, provided you avoid two dangers, either of sensational exaggeration—trying to work things up and make melodramatic sins out of small matters—or the opposite danger of slurring things over. It is essential to use the plain, simple old-fashioned words that you would use about anyone else. I mean words like theft, or fornication, or hatred, instead of "I did not mean to be dishonest," or "I was only a boy then," or "I lost my temper." I think that this steady facing of what one does know and bringing it before God, without excuses, and seriously asking for Forgiveness and Grace, and resolving as far as in one lies to do better, is the only way in which we can ever begin to know the fatal thing which is always there, and preventing us from becoming perfectly just to our wife or husband, or being a better employer or employee. If this process is gone through, I do not doubt that most of us will come to understand and to share these old words like "contrite", "miserable" and "intolerable".

Does that sound very gloomy? Does Christianity encourage morbid introspection? The alternative is much more morbid. Those who do not think about their own sins make up for it by thinking incessantly about the sins of others. It is healthier to think of one's own. It is the reverse of morbid. It is not even, in the long run, very gloomy. A serious attempt to repent and really to know one's own sins is in the long run a lightening and relieving process. Of course, there is bound to be a first dismay and often terror and later great pain, yet that is much less in the long run than the anguish of a mass of unrepented and unexamined sins, lurking the background of our minds. It is the difference between the pain of the tooth about which you should go to the dentist, and the simple straight-forward pain which you know is getting less and less every moment when you have had the tooth out.

WHAT ARE TIPS FOR
AVOIDING GOD AND
PRAYER ALTOGETHER?
(A DEVIL'S PERSPECTIVE)

Editor's Note: In The Screwtape Letters, *Lewis wrote in the character of a demonic master tempter named Screwtape advising a younger demon, Wormwood, who is in charge of tempting a particular human being, and so the reader is expected to do some translating (such as "the Enemy" meaning God) to benefit from this insightful examination of how our souls function.*

PART I: MAKE SURE YOUR PRAYERS ARE ESPECIALLY "SPIRITUAL"

MY DEAR WORMWOOD,

. . . It is, no doubt, impossible to prevent his praying for his mother, but we have means of rendering the prayers innocuous. Make sure that they are always very 'spiritual', that he is always concerned with the state of her soul and never with her rheumatism. Two advantages will follow. In the first place, his attention will be kept on what he regards as her sins, by which, with a little guidance from you, he can be induced to mean any of her actions which are inconvenient or

The Screwtape Letters (from chapter 3).

irritating to himself. Thus you can keep rubbing the wounds of the day a little sorer even while he is on his knees; the operation is not at all difficult and you will find it very entertaining. In the second place, since his ideas about her soul will be very crude and often erroneous, he will, in some degree, be praying for an imaginary person, and it will be your task to make that imaginary person daily less and less like the real mother—the sharp-tongued old lady at the breakfast table. In time, you may get the cleavage so wide that no thought or feeling from his prayers for the imagined mother will ever flow over into his treatment of the real one. I have had patients of my own so well in hand that they could be turned at a moment's notice from impassioned prayer for a wife's or son's 'soul' to beating or insulting the real wife or son without a qualm. . . .

The amateurish suggestions in your last letter warn me that it is high time for me to write to you fully on the painful subject of prayer. You might have spared the comment that my advice about his prayers for his mother 'proved singularly unfortunate'. That is not the sort of thing that a nephew should write to his uncle—nor a junior tempter to the under-secretary of a department. It also reveals an unpleasant desire to shift responsibility; you must learn to pay for your own blunders.

The best thing, where it is possible, is to keep the patient from the serious intention of praying altogether. When the patient is an adult recently reconverted to the Enemy's party, like your man, this is best done by encouraging him to remember, or to think he remembers, the parrot-like nature of his prayers in childhood. In reaction against that, he may be persuaded to aim at something entirely spontaneous, inward, informal, and unregularised; and what this will actually mean to a beginner will be an effort to produce in himself a vaguely devotional *mood* in which real concentration of will and intelligence have no part. One of their poets, Coleridge, has recorded that he did not pray 'with moving lips and bended knees' but merely 'composed his spirit to love' and

From all my lame defeats and oh! much more
From all the victories that I seemed to score;
From cleverness shot forth on Thy behalf
At which, while angels weep, the audience
   laugh;
From all my proofs of Thy divinity,
Thou, who wouldst give no sign, deliver me.

Thoughts are but coins. Let me not trust,
   instead
Of Thee, their thin-worn image of Thy head.
From all my thoughts, even from my thoughts
   of Thee,
O thou fair Silence, fall, and set me free.
Lord of the narrow gate and the needle's eye,
Take from me all my trumpery lest I die.

—"THE APOLOGIST'S EVENING PRAYER," *POEMS*

indulged 'a sense of supplication'. That is exactly the sort of prayer we want; and since it bears a superficial resemblance to the prayer of silence as practised by those who are very far advanced in the Enemy's service, clever and lazy patients can be taken in by it for quite a long time. At the very least, they can be persuaded that the bodily position makes no difference to their prayers; for they constantly forget, what you must always remember, that they are animals and that whatever their bodies do affects their souls. It is funny how mortals always picture us as putting things into their minds: in reality our best work is done by keeping things out.

If this fails, you must fall back on a subtler misdirection of his intention. Whenever they are attending to the Enemy Himself we are defeated, but there are ways of preventing them from doing so. The simplest is to turn their gaze away from Him towards themselves. Keep them watching their own minds and trying to produce *feelings* there by the action of their own wills. When they meant to ask Him for charity, let them, instead, start trying to manufacture charitable feelings for themselves and not notice that this is what they are doing. When they meant to pray for courage, let them really be trying to feel brave. When they say they are praying for forgiveness, let them be trying to feel forgiven. Teach them to estimate the value of each prayer by their success in producing the desired feeling; and never let them suspect how much success or failure of that kind depends on whether they are well or ill, fresh or tired, at the moment.

But of course the Enemy will not meantime be idle. Whenever there is prayer, there is danger of His own immediate action. He is cynically indifferent to the dignity of His position, and ours, as pure spirits, and to human animals on their knees He pours out self-knowledge in a quite shameless fashion. But even if He defeats your first attempt at misdirection, we have a subtler weapon. The humans do not start from that direct perception of Him which we, unhappily, cannot avoid. They have never known that ghastly luminosity, that stabbing and searing glare which makes the background of permanent pain to our lives. If you look into your patient's mind when he is praying, you will not find *that*. If you examine the object to which he is attending, you will find that it is a composite object containing many quite ridiculous ingredients. There will be images derived from pictures of the Enemy as He appeared during the discreditable episode known as the Incarnation: there will be vaguer—perhaps quite savage and puerile—images associated with the other two Persons. There will even be some of his own reverence (and of bodily sensations accompanying it) objectified and attributed to the object revered. I have known cases where what the patient called his 'God' was actually *located*—up and to the left at the corner of the bedroom ceiling, or inside his own head, or in a crucifix on the wall. But whatever the nature of the composite object, you must keep him praying to *it*—to the thing that he has made, not to the Person who has made him. You may even encourage him to attach great importance to the correction and improvement of his composite object, and to keeping it steadily before his imagination during the whole prayer. For if he ever comes to make the distinction, if ever he consciously directs his prayers 'Not to what

I think thou art but to what thou knowest thyself to be', our situation is, for the moment, desperate. Once all his thoughts and images have been flung aside or, if retained, retained with a full recognition of their merely subjective nature, and the man trusts himself to the completely real, external, invisible Presence, there with him in the room and never knowable by him as he is known by it—why, then it is that the incalculable may occur. In avoiding this situation— this real nakedness of the soul in prayer—you will be helped by the fact that the humans themselves do not desire it as much as they suppose. There's such a thing as getting more than they bargained for!

PART 2: BELIEVE YOU ARE NOT
A VERY GOOD CHRISTIAN

MY DEAR WORMWOOD,

. . . I am almost glad to hear that he is still a church-goer and a communicant. I know there are dangers in this; but anything is better than that he should realise the break he has made with the first months of his Christian life. As long as he retains externally the habits of a Christian he can still be made to think of himself as one who has adopted a few new friends and amusements but whose spiritual state is much the same as it was six weeks ago. And while he thinks that,

---

The Screwtape Letters (from chapter 12).

we do not have to contend with the explicit repentance of a definite, fully recognised, sin, but only with his vague, though uneasy, feeling that he hasn't been doing very well lately.

This dim uneasiness needs careful handling. If it gets too strong it may wake him up and spoil the whole game. On the other hand, if you suppress it entirely—which, by the by, the Enemy will probably not allow you to do—we lose an element in the situation which can be turned to good account. If such a feeling is allowed to live, but not allowed to become irresistible and flower into real repentance, it has one invaluable tendency. It increases the patient's reluctance to think about the Enemy. All humans at nearly all times have some such reluctance; but when thinking of Him involves facing and intensifying a whole vague cloud of half-conscious guilt, this reluctance is increased tenfold. They hate every idea that suggests Him, just as men in financial embarrassment hate the very sight of a pass-book. In this state your patient will not omit, but he will increasingly dislike, his religious duties. He will think about them as little as he feels he decently can beforehand, and forget them as soon as possible when they are over. A few weeks ago you had to *tempt* him to unreality and inattention in his prayers: but now you will find him opening his arms to you and almost begging you to distract his purpose and benumb his heart. He will *want* his prayers to be unreal, for he will dread nothing so much as effective

"Hence the prayers offered in the state of dryness are those which please Him best. We can drag our patients along by continual tempting, because we design them only for the table, and the more their will is interfered with the better. He cannot 'tempt' to virtue as we do to vice. He wants them to learn to walk and must therefore take away His hand; and if only the will to walk is really there He is pleased even with their stumbles."

—*THE SCREWTAPE LETTERS*

contact with the Enemy. His aim will be to let sleeping worms lie.

As this condition becomes more fully established, you will be gradually freed from the tiresome business of providing Pleasures as temptations. As the uneasiness and his reluctance to face it cut him off more and more from all real happiness, and as habit renders the pleasures of vanity and excitement and flippancy at once less pleasant and harder to forgo (for that is what habit fortunately does to a pleasure) you will find that anything or nothing is sufficient to attract his wandering attention. You no longer need a good book, which he really likes, to keep him from his prayers or his work or his sleep; a column of advertisements in yesterday's paper will do. You can make him waste his time not only in conversation he enjoys with people whom he likes, but in conversations with those he cares nothing about on subjects that bore him. You can make him do nothing at all for long periods. You can keep him up late at night, not roistering, but staring at a dead fire in a cold room. All the healthy and out-going activities which we want him to avoid can be inhibited and *nothing* given in return, so that at least he may say, as one of my own patients said on his arrival down here, 'I now see that I spent most of my life in doing *neither* what I ought *nor* what I liked.' The Christians describe the Enemy as one 'without whom Nothing is strong'. And Nothing is very strong: strong enough to steal away a man's best years not in sweet sins but in a dreary flickering of the mind over it knows not what and knows not why, in the gratification of curiosities so feeble that the man is only half aware of them, in drumming of fingers and kicking of heels, in whistling tunes that he does not like, or in the long, dim labyrinth of reveries that have not even lust or ambition to give them a relish, but which, once chance association has started them, the creature is too weak and fuddled to shake off.

You will say that these are very small sins; and doubtless, like all young tempters, you are anxious to be able to report spectacular wickedness. But do remember, the only thing that matters is the extent to which you separate the man from the Enemy. It does not matter how small the sins are provided that their cumulative effect is to edge the man away from the Light and out into the Nothing. Murder is no better than cards if cards can do the trick. Indeed the safest road to Hell is the gradual one—the gentle slope, soft underfoot, without sudden turnings, without milestones, without signposts.

PART 3: TREAT PRAYERS AS TESTS OF GOD

MY DEAR WORMWOOD,

You seem to be doing very little good at present. The use of his 'love' to distract his mind from the Enemy is, of course, obvious, but you reveal what poor use you are making of it when you say that the whole question of distraction and the wandering mind has now become one of the chief subjects of his prayers. That means you have largely failed. When this, or any other distraction, crosses his mind you ought to encourage him to thrust it away by sheer will power and to try to continue the normal prayer as if noth-

---

The Screwtape Letters (from chapter 27).

ing had happened; once he accepts the distraction as his present problem and lays *that* before the Enemy and makes it the main theme of his prayers and his endeavours, then, so far from doing good, you have done harm. Anything, even a sin, which has the total effect of moving him close up to the Enemy, makes against us in the long run.

A promising line is the following. Now that he is in love, a new idea of *earthly* happiness has arisen in his mind: and hence a new urgency in his purely petitionary prayers—about this war and other such matters. Now is the time for raising intellectual difficulties about prayer of that sort. False spirituality is always to be encouraged. On the seemingly pious ground that 'praise and communion with God is the true prayer', humans can often be lured into direct disobedience to the Enemy who (in His usual flat, commonplace, uninteresting way) has definitely told them to pray for their daily bread and the recovery of their sick. You will, of course, conceal from him the fact that the prayer for daily bread, interpreted in a 'spiritual sense', is really just as crudely petitionary as it is in any other sense.

But since your patient has contracted the terrible habit of obedience, he will probably continue such 'crude' prayers whatever you do. But you can worry him with the haunting suspicion that the practice is absurd and can have no objective result. Don't forget to use the 'heads I win, tails you lose' argument. If the thing he prays for doesn't happen, then that is one more proof that petitionary prayers don't work; if it does happen, he will, of course, be able to see some of the physical causes which led up to it, and 'therefore it would have happened anyway', and thus a granted prayer becomes just as good a proof as a denied one that prayers are ineffective.

You, being a spirit, will find it difficult to understand how he gets into this confusion. But you must remember that he takes Time for an ultimate reality. He supposes that the Enemy, like himself, sees some things as present, remembers others as past, and anticipates others as future; or even if he believes that the Enemy does not see things that way, yet, in his heart of hearts, he regards this as a peculiarity of the Enemy's mode of perception—he doesn't really think (though he would say he did) that things as the Enemy sees them are things as they are! If you tried to explain to him that men's prayers today are one of the innumerable co-ordinates with which the Enemy harmonises the weather of tomorrow, he would reply that then the Enemy always knew men were going to make those prayers and, if so, they did not pray freely but were predestined to do so. And he would add that the weather on a given day can be traced back through its causes to the original creation of matter itself—so that the whole thing, both on the human and on the material side, is given 'from the word go'. What he ought to say, of course, is obvious to us; that the problem of adapting the particular weather to the particular prayers is merely the appearance, at two points in his temporal mode of perception, of the total problem of adapting the whole spiritual universe to the whole corporeal universe; that creation in its entirety operates at every point of space and time, or rather that their kind of consciousness forces them to encounter the whole, self-consistent creative act as a series of successive events. *Why* that creative act leaves room for their free will is the problem of problems, the se-cret behind the Enemy's nonsense about 'Love'. *How* it does so is no problem at all; for the Enemy does not *foresee* the humans making their free contributions in a future, but *sees* them doing so in His unbounded Now. And obviously to watch a man doing something is not to make him do it.

❧

PART 4: FOCUS ON YOUR OWN STATE OF MIND

MY DEAR WORMWOOD,

... There is nothing like suspense and anxiety for barricading a human's mind against the Enemy. He wants men to be concerned with what they do; our business is to keep them thinking about what will happen to them.

Your patient will, of course, have picked up the notion that he must submit with patience to the Enemy's will. What the Enemy means by this is primarily that he should accept with patience the tribulation which has actually been dealt out to him—the present

---

The Screwtape Letters (from chapter 6).

anxiety and suspense. It is about *this* that he is to say 'Thy will be done', and for the daily task of bearing *this* that the daily bread will be provided. It is your business to see that the patient never thinks of the present fear as his appointed cross, but only of the things he is afraid of. Let him regard them as his crosses: let him forget that, since they are incompatible, they cannot all happen to him, and let him try to practise fortitude and patience to them all in advance. For real resignation, at the same moment, to a dozen different and hypothetical fates, is almost impossible, and the Enemy does not greatly assist those who are trying to attain it: resignation to present and actual suffering, even where that suffering consists of fear, is easier and is usually helped by this direct action.

An important spiritual law is here involved. I have explained that you can weaken his prayers by diverting his attention from the Enemy Himself to his own states of mind about the Enemy. On the other hand, fear becomes easier to master when the patient's mind is diverted from the thing feared to the fear itself, considered as a present and undesirable state of his own mind; and when he regards the fear as his appointed cross he will inevitably think of it as a state of mind. One can therefore formulate the general rule; in all activities of mind which favour our cause, encourage the patient to be unself-conscious and to concentrate on the object, but in all activities favourable to the Enemy bend his mind back on itself. Let an insult or a woman's body so fix his attention outward that he does not reflect 'I am now entering into the state called Anger—or the state called Lust.' Contrariwise let the reflection 'My feelings are now growing more devout, or more charitable' so fix his attention inward that he no longer looks beyond himself to see our Enemy or his own neighbours.

HOW DOES PRAYER BECOME A REGULAR PRACTICE FOR US?

DEAR MRS. _____,

I have been praying for you daily, as always, but latterly have found myself doing so with much more concern and especially about 2 nights ago, with such a strong feeling how very nice it would be, if God willed, to get a letter from you with good news. And then, as if by magic (indeed it is the whitest magic in the world) the letter comes to-day. Not (lest I should indulge in folly) that your relief had not in fact occurred before my prayer, but as if, in tenderness for

---

From *Letters to an American Lady*.

my puny faith God moved me to pray with espe-
cial earnestness just before He was going to give me
the thing. How true that our prayers are really His
prayers; He speaks to Himself through us. . . .

I don't think we ought to try to keep up our normal
prayers when we are ill and over-tired. I would not say
this to a beginner who still has the habit to form. But
you are past that stage. One mustn't make the Christian life into a punctilious system of law . . . [for] two
reasons (1) It raises scruples when we don't keep the
routine (2) It raises presumption when we do. Nothing gives one a more spuriously good conscience than
keeping rules, even if there has been a total absence of
all real charity and faith. And people who stay away
from Mass with the approval of their director and at
the bidding of their doctor are just as obedient as those
who go. Check all these points with your confessor: I
bet he'll say just the same. And of course the presence
of God is not the same as the sense of the presence of
God. The latter may be due to imagination; the former
may be attended with no "sensible consolation". The

❧

"Say your prayers in a garden early, ignoring steadfastly the dew, the birds and the flowers, and you will come away overwhelmed by its freshness and joy; go there in order to be overwhelmed and, after a certain age, nine times out of ten nothing will happen to you."

—*THE FOUR LOVES*

Father was not really absent from the Son when He said "Why hast thou forsaken me?" You see God Himself, as man, submitted to man's sense of being abandoned. The real parallel on the natural level is one which seems odd for a bachelor to write to a lady, but too illuminating not to be used. The act which engenders a child ought to be, and usually is attended by pleasure. But it is not the pleasure that produces the child. Where there is pleasure there may be sterility: where there is no pleasure the act may be fertile. And in the spiritual marriage of God and the soul it is the same. It is the actual presence, not the sensation of the presence, of the

Holy Ghost which begets Christ in us. The *sense* of the presence is a super-added gift for which we give thanks when it comes, and that's all about it. . . .

We all go through periods of dryness in our prayers, don't we? I doubt (but ask your *directeur*) whether they are necessarily a bad symptom. I sometimes suspect that what we *feel* to be our best prayers are really our worst; that what we are enjoying is the satisfaction of apparent success, as in executing a dance or reciting a poem. Do our prayers sometimes go wrong because we insist on trying to talk to God when He wants to talk to us? Joy tells me that once, years ago, she was haunted one morning by a feeling that God wanted something of her, a persistent pressure like the nag of a neglected duty. And till mid-morning she kept on wondering what it was. But the moment she stopped worrying, the answer came through as plain as a spoken voice. It was "I don't want you to *do* anything. I want to *give* you something"; and immediately her heart was full of peace and delight. St. Augustine says "God gives where He finds empty hands". A man whose hands are full of parcels can't receive a gift. Perhaps these parcels are not always sins or earthly cares, but sometimes our own fussy attempts to worship Him in *our* way. Incidentally, what most often interrupts my own prayers is not great distractions but tiny ones—things one will have to do or avoid in the course of the next hour. . . .

Yes—it is sometimes hard to obey St. Paul's "Rejoice". We must try to take life moment by moment. The actual *present* is usually pretty tolerable, I think, if only we refrain from adding to its burden that of the past and the future. How right Our Lord is about "sufficient to the day". Do even pious people in their reverence for the more radiantly divine element in His sayings, sometimes attend too little to their sheer practical common-sense? . . .

Let us by all means pray for one another: it is perhaps the only form of "work for re-union" which never does anything but good. God bless you.

Yours most sincerely,

C. S. LEWIS

HOW CAN WE GET OUT OF OUR OWN WAY AND PRAY?

NOT LONG AGO when I was using the collect for the fourth Sunday after Trinity in my private prayers I found that I had made a slip of the tongue. I had meant to pray that I might so pass through things temporal that I finally lost not the things eternal; I found I had prayed so to pass through things eternal that I finally lost not the things temporal. Of course I don't think that a slip of the tongue is a sin. I am not sure that I am even a strict enough Freudian to believe that all such slips, without exception, are deeply significant. But I think some of them are significant, and I thought this

---

The Weight of Glory (from "A Slip of the Tongue").

was one of that sort. I thought that what I had inadvertently said very nearly expressed something I had really wished.

Very nearly; not, of course, precisely. I had never been quite stupid enough to think that the eternal could, strictly, be 'passed through'. What I had wanted to pass through without prejudice to my things temporal was those hours or moments in which I attended to the eternal, in which I exposed myself to it.

I mean this sort of thing. I say my prayers, I read a book of devotion, I prepare for, or receive, the Sacrament. But while I do these things there is, so to speak, a voice inside me that urges caution. It tells me to be careful; to keep my head; not to go too far; not to burn my boats. I come into the presence of God with a great fear lest anything should happen to me within that presence which will prove too intolerably inconvenient when I have come out again into my 'ordinary' life. I don't want to be carried away into any resolution which I shall afterwards regret. For I know I shall be feeling quite different after breakfast;

I don't want anything to happen to me at the altar which will run up too big a bill to pay then. It would be very disagreeable, for instance, to take the duty of charity (while I am at the altar) so seriously that, after breakfast, I had to tear up the really stunning reply I had written to an impudent correspondent yesterday and meant to post today. It would be very tiresome to commit myself to a programme of temperance which would cut off my after-breakfast cigarette (or, at best, make it cruelly alternative to a cigarette later in the morning). Even repentance of past acts will have to be paid for. By repenting one acknowledges them as sins—therefore not to be repeated. Better leave that issue undecided.

The root principle of all these precautions is the same: to guard the things temporal. And I find some evidence that this temptation is not peculiar to me. A good author (whose name I have forgotten) asks somewhere, 'Have we never risen from our knees in haste for fear God's will should become too unmistakable if we prayed longer?' The following story was told as true. An Irish woman who had just been at confession met on the steps of the chapel the other woman who was her greatest enemy in the village. The other woman let fly a torrent of abuse. 'Isn't it a shame for ye,' replied Biddy, 'to be talking to me like that, ye coward, and me in a state of Grace the way I can't answer ye? But you wait. I won't be in a state of Grace long.' There is an excellent tragi-comic example in Trollope's *Last Chronicle*. The Archdeacon was angry with his eldest son. He at once made a number of legal arrangements to the son's disadvantage. They could all easily have been made a few days later,

> Pitch your demands heaven-high and they'll
>   be met.
> Ask for the Morning Star and take (thrown in)
> Your earthly love. Why, yes; but how to set
> One's foot on the first rung, how to begin?
>
> —"FIVE SONNETS," *POEMS*

but Trollope explains why the Archdeacon would not wait. To reach the next day, he had to pass through his evening prayers, and he knew that he might not be able to carry his hostile plans safely through the clause, 'Forgive us our trespasses as we forgive.' So he got in first, he decided to present God with a *fait accompli*. This is an extreme case of the precautions I am talking about; the man will not venture within reach of the eternal until he has made the things temporal safe in advance.

This is my endlessly recurrent temptation: to go down to that sea (I think St. John of the Cross called God a sea) and there neither dive nor swim nor float, but only dabble and splash, careful not to get out of my depth and holding on to the lifeline which connects me with my things temporal.

It is different from the temptations that met us at the beginning of the Christian life. Then we fought (at least I fought) against admitting the claims of the eternal at all. And when we had fought, and been beaten, and surrendered, we supposed that all would be fairly plain sailing. This temptation comes later. It is addressed to those who have already admitted the claim in principle and are even making some sort of effort to meet it. Our temptation is to look eagerly for the minimum that will be accepted. We are in fact very like honest but reluctant taxpayers. We approve of an income tax in principle. We make our returns truthfully. But we dread a rise in the tax. We are very careful to pay no more than is necessary. And we hope—we very ardently hope—that after we have paid it there will still be enough left to live on.

And notice that those cautions which the tempter whispers in our ears are all plausible. Indeed, I don't think he often tries to deceive us (after early youth) with a direct lie. The plausibility is this. It is really possible to be carried away by religious emotion— *enthusiasm* as our ancestors called it—into resolutions and attitudes which we shall, not sinfully but rationally, not when we are more worldly but when we are wiser, have cause to regret. We can become scrupulous or fanatical; we can, in what seems zeal but is really presumption, embrace tasks never intended for us. That is the truth in the temptation. The lie consists in the suggestion that our best protection is a prudent regard for the safety of our pocket, our habitual indulgences, and our ambitions. But that is quite false. Our real protection is to be sought elsewhere; in common Christian usage, in moral theology, in steady rational thinking, in the advice of good friends and good books, and (if need be) in a skilled spiritual director. Swimming lessons are better than a lifeline to the shore.

For of course that lifeline is really a death-line. There is no parallel to paying taxes and living on the remainder. For it is not so much of our time and so much of our attention that God demands; it is not even all our time and all our attention: it is ourselves. For each of us the Baptist's words are true: 'He must increase and I decrease.' He will be infinitely merciful to our repeated failures; I know no promise that He will accept a deliberate compromise. For He has, in the last resort, nothing to give us but Himself; and

He can give that only in so far as our self-affirming will retires and makes room for Him in our souls. Let us make up our minds to it; there will be nothing 'of our own' left over to live on; no 'ordinary' life. I do not mean that each of us will necessarily be called to be a martyr or even an ascetic. That's as may be. For some (nobody knows which) the Christian life will include much leisure, many occupations we naturally like. But these will be received from God's hands. In a perfect Christian they would be as much part of his 'religion', his 'service', as his hardest duties, and his feasts would be as Christian as his fasts. What cannot be admitted—what must exist only as an undefeated but daily resisted enemy—is the idea of something that is 'our own', some area in which we are to be 'out of school', on which God has no claim.

For he claims all, because He is love and must bless. He cannot bless us unless He has us. When we try to keep within us an area that is our own, we try to keep an area of death. Therefore, in love, He claims all. There's no bargaining with Him.

This is, I take it, the meaning of all those sayings that alarm me most. Thomas More said, 'If ye make indentures with God how much ye will serve Him, ye shall find ye have signed both of them yourself.' Law, in his terrible, cool voice, said, 'Many will be rejected at the last day, not because they have taken no time or pains about their salvation, but because they have not taken time and pains enough'; and later, in his richer, Behmenite period, 'If you have not chosen the Kingdom of God, it will make in the end no difference what you have chosen instead.' Those are hard words to take. Will it really make no difference whether it was women or patriotism, cocaine or art, whisky or a seat in the Cabinet, money or science? Well, surely no difference that matters. We shall have missed the end for which we are formed and rejected the only thing that satisfies. Does it matter to a man dying in a desert, by which choice of route he missed the only well?

HOW DO WE MAKE SURE IT IS THE REAL "I" WHO STANDS BEFORE THE REAL "THOU" IN PRAYER?

THE MOMENT OF prayer is for me—or involves for me as its condition—the awareness, the re-awakened awareness, that this 'real world' and 'real self' are very far from being rock bottom realities. I cannot, in the flesh, leave the stage, either to go behind the scenes or to take my seat in the pit; but I can remember that these regions exist. And I also remember that my apparent self—this clown or hero or super—under his grease-paint is a real person with an off-

Letters to Malcolm (from chapter 15).

He whom I bow to only knows to whom I bow
When I attempt the ineffable Name, murmuring
   Thou,
And dream of Pheidian fancies and embrace in
   heart
Symbols (I know) which cannot be the thing
   Thou art.
Thus always, taken at their word, all prayers
   blaspheme
Worshipping with frail images a folk-lore dream,
And all men in their praying, self-deceived,
   address
The coinage of their own unquiet thoughts, unless
Thou in magnetic mercy to Thyself divert
Our arrows, aimed unskilfully, beyond desert;
And all men are idolators, crying unheard
To a deaf idol, if Thou take them at their word.
Take not, oh Lord, our literal sense. Lord, in Thy
   great,
Unbroken speech our limping metaphor translate.

—"FOOTNOTE TO ALL PRAYERS," *POEMS*

stage life. The dramatic person could not tread the stage unless he concealed a real person: unless the real and unknown I existed, I would not even make mistakes about the imagined me. And in prayer this real I struggles to speak, for once, from his real being, and to address, for once, not the other actors, but—what shall I call Him? The Author, for He invented us all? The Producer, for He controls all? Or the Audience, for He watches, and will judge, the performance?

The attempt is not to escape from space and time and from my creaturely situation as a subject facing objects. It is more modest: to re-awake the awareness of that situation. If that can be done, there is no need to go anywhere else. This situation itself is, at every moment, a possible theophany. Here is the holy ground; the Bush is burning now.

Of course this attempt may be attended with almost every degree of success or failure. The prayer preceding all prayers is 'May it be the real I who speaks. May it be the real Thou that I speak to.' Infinitely various are the levels from which we pray. Emotional

> All those expressions of unworthiness which Christian practice puts into the believer's mouth seem to the outer world like the degraded and insincere grovellings of a sycophant before a tyrant, or at best a façon de parler like the self-depreciation of a Chinese gentleman when he calls himself "this coarse and illiterate person". In reality, however, they express the continually renewed, because continually necessary, attempt to negate that misconception of ourselves and of our relation to God which nature, even while we pray, is always recommending to us. No sooner do we believe that God loves us than there is an impulse to believe that He does so, not because He is Love, but because we are intrinsically lovable.
>
> —*THE FOUR LOVES*

intensity is in itself no proof of spiritual depth. If we pray in terror we shall pray earnestly; it only proves that terror is an earnest emotion. Only God Himself can let the bucket down to the depths in us. And, on the other side, He must constantly work as the iconoclast. Every idea of Him we form, He must in mercy shatter. The most blessed result of prayer would be to rise thinking 'But I never knew before. I never dreamed . . .' I suppose it was at such a moment that Thomas Aquinas said of all his own theology, 'It reminds me of straw.'

HOW CAN WE BE LIKE DAVID AND PRAY WITH DELIGHT?

THE MOST VALUABLE thing the Psalms do for me is to express that same delight in God which made David dance. I am not saying that this is so pure or so profound a thing as the love of God reached by the greatest Christian saints and mystics. But I am not comparing it with that, I am comparing it with the merely dutiful "church-going" and laborious "saying our prayers" to which most of us are, thank God not always, but often, reduced. Against that it stands out as something astonishingly robust, virile, and

---

Reflections on the Psalms (from chapter 5, "The Fair Beauty of the Lord").

spontaneous; something we may regard with an innocent envy and may hope to be infected by as we read.

For the reason I have given this delight is very much centred on the Temple. The simpler poets do not in fact distinguish between the love of God in what we might (rather dangerously) call "a spiritual sense" and their enjoyment of the festivals in the Temple. We must not misunderstand this. The Jews were not, like the Greeks, an analytical and logical people; indeed, except the Greeks, no ancient peoples were. The sort of distinction which we can easily make between those who are really worshipping God in church and those who enjoy "a beautiful service" for musical, antiquarian, or merely sentimental reasons, would have been impossible to them. We get nearest to their state of mind if we think of a pious modern farm-labourer at church on Christmas Day or at the harvest thanksgiving. I mean, of course, one who really believes, who is a regular communicant; not one who goes only on these occasions and is thus (not in the worst but in the best sense of that word) a Pagan, practising Pagan piety, making his bow to the Unknown—and at other times Forgotten—on the great annual festivals. The man I picture is a real Christian. But you would do him wrong by asking him to separate out, at such moments, some exclusively religious element in his mind from all the rest—from his hearty social pleasure in a corporate act, his enjoyment of the hymns (and the crowd), his memory of other such services since childhood, his well-earned anticipation of rest after harvest or Christmas dinner after church. They are all one in his mind. This would have been even truer of any ancient man, and especially of an ancient Jew. He was a peasant, very close to the soil. He had never heard of music, or festivity, or agriculture as things separate from religion, nor of religion as something separate from them. Life was one. This of course laid him open to spiritual dangers which more sophisticated people can avoid; it also gave him privileges which they lack.

Thus when the Psalmists speak of "seeing" the Lord, or long to "see" Him, most of them mean something that happened to them in the Temple. The fatal way of putting this would be to say "they only mean they have seen the festival". It would be better to say "If we had been there we should have seen only the festival". Thus in 68 "It is well seen, O God, how thou goest . . . in the sanctuary . . . the singers go before, the minstrels follow after; in the midst are the damsels playing with the timbrels" (68:24, 25), it is almost as if the poet said "Look, here He comes". If I had been there I should have seen the musicians and the girls with the tambourines; in addition, as another thing, I might or might not have (as we say) "felt" the presence of God. The ancient worshipper would have been aware of no such dualism. Similarly, if a modern man wished to "dwell in the house of the Lord all the days of his life, to behold the fair beauty of the Lord" (27:4) he would mean, I suppose, that he hoped to receive, not of course without the mediation of the sacraments and the help of other "services", but as something distinguishable from them and not to be presumed upon as their inevitable result, frequent moments of spiritual vision and the "sensible" love of God. But I suspect that the poet of that Psalm drew no distinction between "beholding the fair beauty of the Lord" and the acts of worship themselves.

When the mind becomes more capable of abstraction and analysis this old unity breaks up. And no sooner is it possible to distinguish the rite from the vision of God than there is a danger of the rite becoming a substitute for, and a rival to, God Himself. Once it can be thought of separately, it will; and it may then take on a rebellious, cancerous life of its own. There is a stage in a child's life at which it cannot separate the religious from the merely festal char-

You're not David and no one has told you to fight Goliath. You've only just enlisted. Don't go off challenging enemy champions. Learn your drill.

—*COLLECTED LETTERS*, MAY 15, 1952, TO MRS. SONIA GRAHAM FROM MAGDALEN COLLEGE

acter of Christmas or Easter. I have been told of a very small and very devout boy who was heard murmuring to himself on Easter morning a poem of his own composition which began "Chocolate eggs and Jesus risen". This seems to me, for his age, both admirable poetry and admirable piety. But of course the time will soon come when such a child can no longer effortlessly and spontaneously enjoy that unity. He will become able to distinguish the spiritual from the ritual and festal aspect of Easter; chocolate eggs will no longer be sacramental. And once he has distinguished he must put one or the other first. If he puts the spiritual first he can still taste something of Easter in the chocolate eggs; if he puts the eggs first they will soon be no more than any other sweetmeat. They have taken on an independent, and therefore a soon withering, life. Either at some period in Judaism, or else in the experience of some Jews, a roughly parallel situation occurred. The unity falls apart; the sacrificial rites become distinguishable from the meeting with God. This does not unfortunately mean that they will cease or become less important. They may, in various evil modes, become even more important than before. They may be valued as a sort of commercial transaction with a greedy God who somehow really wants or needs large quantities of carcasses and whose favours cannot be secured on any other terms. Worse still, they may be regarded as the only thing He wants, so that their punctual performance will satisfy Him without obedience to His demands for mercy, "judgement", and truth. To the priests themselves the whole system will seem important simply because it is both their art and their livelihood; all their pedantry, all their pride, all their economic position, is bound up with it. They will elaborate their art more and more. And of course the corrective to these views of sacrifice can be found within Judaism itself. The prophets continually fulminate against it. Even the Psalter, though largely a Temple collection, can do so; as in Psalm 50 where God tells His people that all this Temple worship, considered in itself, is not the real point at all, and particularly ridicules the genu-

> ✎
>
> Almighty God, who art the father of lights and who has promised by thy dear Son that all who do thy will shall know thy doctrine: give me grace so to live that by daily obedience I daily increase in faith and in the understanding of thy Holy Word, through Jesus Christ our Lord.
>
> —COLLECTED LETTERS, MARCH 18, 1952

inely Pagan notion that He really needs to be fed with roast meat. "If I were hungry, do you think I would apply to *you*?" (50:12). I have sometimes fancied He might similarly ask a certain type of modern clergyman, "If I wanted music—if I were conducting research into the more recondite details of the history of the Western Rite—do you really think *you* are the source I would rely on?"

This possible degradation of sacrifice and the rebukes of it are, however, so well known that there is no need to stress them here. I want to stress what I think that we (or at least I) need more; the joy and delight in God which meet us in the Psalms, however loosely or closely, in this or that instance, they may be connected with the Temple. This is the living centre of Judaism. These poets knew far less reason than we for loving God. They did not know that He offered them eternal joy; still less that He would die to win it for them. Yet they express a longing for Him, for His mere presence, which comes only to the best Christians or to Christians in their best moments. They long to live all their days in the Temple so that they may constantly see "the fair beauty of the Lord" (27:4). Their longing to go up to Jerusalem and "appear before the presence of God" is like a physical thirst (42). From Jerusalem His presence flashes out "in perfect beauty" (50:2). Lacking that encounter with Him, their souls are parched like a waterless countryside (63:2). They crave to be "satisfied with the pleasures" of His house (65:4). Only there can they be at ease, like a bird in the nest (84:3). One day of those "pleasures" is better than a lifetime spent elsewhere (84:10).

I have rather—though the expression may seem harsh to some—called this the "appetite for God" than "the love of God". The "love of God" too easily suggests the word "spiritual" in all those negative or restrictive senses which it has unhappily acquired. These old poets do not seem to think that they are meritorious or pious for having such feelings; nor, on the other hand, that they are privileged in being given the grace to have them. They are at once less priggish about it than the worst of us and less humble—one might almost say, less surprised—than the best of us. It has all the cheerful spontaneity of a natural, even a physical, desire. It is gay and jocund. They are glad and rejoice (9:2). Their fingers itch for the harp (43:4), for the lute and the harp—wake up, lute and harp!—(57:9); let's have a song, bring the tambourine, bring the "merry harp with the lute", we're going to sing merrily and make a cheerful noise (81:1, 2). Noise, you may well say. Mere music is not enough. Let everyone, even the benighted gentiles, clap their hands (47:1). Let us have clashing cymbals, not only well tuned, but *loud*, and dances too (150:5). Let even the remote islands (all islands were remote, for the Jews were no sailors) share the exultation (97:1).

I am not saying that this gusto—if you like, this rowdiness—can or should be revived. Some of it cannot be revived because it is not dead but with us still. It would be idle to pretend that we Anglicans are a striking example. The Romans, the Orthodox, and the Salvation Army all, I think, have retained more of it than we. We have a terrible concern about good taste. Yet even we can still exult. The second reason goes far deeper. All Christians know something the Jews did not know about what it "cost to redeem their souls". Our life as Christians begins by being baptised into a death; our most joyous festivals begin with, and centre upon, the broken body and the shed blood. There is thus a tragic depth in our worship which Judaism lacked. Our joy has to be the sort of joy which can coexist with that; there is for us a spiritual counterpoint where they had simple melody. But this does not in the least cancel the delighted debt which I, for one, feel that I owe to the most jocund Psalms. There, despite the presence of elements we should now find it hard to regard as religious at all, and the absence of elements which some might think essential to religion, I find an experience fully God-centred, asking of God no gift more urgently than His presence, the gift of Himself, joyous to the highest degree, and unmistakably real. What I see (so to speak) in the faces of these old poets tells me more about the God whom they and we adore.

HOW DO WE MAKE SENSE OF WHAT THE NEW TESTAMENT TEACHES ABOUT PRAYER?

THE NEW TESTAMENT contains embarrassing promises that what we pray for with faith we shall receive. Mark 11:24 is the most staggering. Whatever we ask for, believing that we'll get it, we'll get. No question, it seems, of confining it to spiritual gifts; *whatever* we ask for. No question of a merely general faith in God, but a belief that you will get the particular thing you ask. No question of getting either it or else something that is really far better for you; you'll get precisely it. And to heap paradox on para-

---

Letters to Malcolm (from chapter 11).

dox, the Greek doesn't even say "believing that you *will* get it". It uses the aorist, ἐλάβετε, which one is tempted to translate "believing that you *got* it". But this final difficulty I shall ignore. I don't expect Aramaic had anything which we—brought up on Latin grammar—would recognise as tenses at all.

How is this astonishing promise to be reconciled—With the observed facts?

With the prayer in Gethsemane, and (as a result of that prayer) the universally accepted view that we should ask everything with a reservation ("if it be Thy will")?

As regards (a), no evasion is possible. Every war, every famine or plague, almost every deathbed, is the monument to a petition that was not granted. At this very moment thousands of people in this one island are facing as a *fait accompli*, the very thing against which they have prayed night and day, pouring out their whole soul in prayer, and, as they thought, with faith. They have sought and not found. They have knocked and it has not been opened. "That which they greatly feared has come upon them."

But (b) though much less often mentioned, is surely an equal difficulty. How is it possible at one and the same moment to have a perfect faith—an untroubled or unhesitating faith as St. James says (I:6)—that you will get what you ask and yet also prepare yourself submissively in advance for a possible refusal? If you envisage a refusal as possible, how can you have simultaneously a perfect confidence that what you ask will not be refused? If you have that confidence, how can you take refusal into account at all?

It is easy to see why so much more is written about worship and contemplation than about "crudely" or "naïvely" petitionary prayer. They may be—I think they are—nobler forms of prayer. But they are also a good deal easier to write about.

As regards the first difficulty, I'm not asking why our petitions are so often refused. Anyone can see in general that this must be so. In our ignorance we ask what is not good for us or for others, or not even intrinsically possible. Or again, to grant one man's prayer involves refusing another's. There is much here which it is hard for our will to accept but nothing that is hard for our intellect to understand. The real problem is different; not why refusal is so frequent, but why the opposite result is so lavishly promised.

Shall we then proceed on Vidler's principles and scrap the embarrassing promises as "venerable archaisms" which have to be "outgrown"? Surely, even if there were no other objection, that method is too easy. If we are free to delete all inconvenient data we

Pray for me, my Father, that I neither persist, through over-boldness, in what is not permitted to me nor withdraw, through too great timidity, from due effort: for he who touches the Ark without authorization and he who, having once put his hand to the plough, draws it back are both lost.

—COLLECTED LETTERS, JANUARY 5, 1953

shall certainly have no theological difficulties; but for the same reason no solutions and no progress. The very writers of the "Tekkies"[detective stories], not to mention the scientists, know better. The troublesome fact, the apparent absurdity which can't be fitted into any synthesis we have yet made, is precisely the one we must not ignore. Ten to one, it's in that covert the fox is lurking. There is always hope if we keep an unsolved problem fairly in view; there's none if we pretend it's not there.

Before going any further, I want to make two purely practical points:

(1) These lavish promises are the worst possible place at which to begin Christian instruction in dealing with a child or a Pagan. You remember what happened when the Widow started Huck Finn off with the idea he could get what he wanted by praying for it. He tried the experiment and then, not unnaturally, never gave Christianity a second thought; we had better not talk about the view of prayer embodied in Mark 11:24 as "naïf" or "elementary". If that passage contains a

truth, it is a truth for very advanced pupils indeed. I
don't think it is "addressed to our condition" (yours
and mine) at all. It is a coping-stone, not a foundation.
For most of us the prayer in Gethsemane is the only
model. Removing mountains can wait.

(2) We must not encourage in ourselves or others
any tendency to work up a subjective state which, if
we succeeded, we should describe as "faith", with the
idea that this will somehow ensure the granting of our
prayer. We have probably all done this as children.
But the state of mind which desperate desire working on a strong imagination can manufacture is not
faith in the Christian sense. It is a feat of psychological gymnastics.

It seems to me we must conclude that such promises about prayer with faith refer to a degree or kind
of faith which most believers never experience. A far
inferior degree is, I hope, acceptable to God. Even the
kind that says, "Help thou my unbelief", may make
way for a miracle. Again, the absence of such faith as
ensures the granting of the prayer is not even neces-

sarily a sin; for Our Lord had no such assurance when He prayed in Gethsemane.

How or why does such faith occur sometimes, but not always, even in the perfect petitioner? We, or I, can only guess. My own idea is that it occurs only when the one who prays does so as God's fellow-worker, demanding what is needed for the joint work. It is the prophet's, the apostle's, the missionary's, the healer's prayer that is made with this confidence and finds the confidence justified by the event. The difference, we are told, between a servant and a friend is that a servant is not in his master's secrets. For him, "orders is orders". He has only his own surmises as to the plans he helps to execute. But the fellow-worker, the companion or (dare we say?) the colleague of God is so united with Him at certain moments that something of the divine foreknowledge enters his mind. Hence his faith is the "evidence"—that is, the evidentness, the obviousness—of things not seen.

As the friend is above the servant, the servant is above the suitor, the man praying on his own behalf.

It is no sin to be a suitor. Our Lord descends into the humiliation of being a suitor, of praying on His own behalf, in Gethsemane. But when He does so the certitude about His Father's will is apparently withdrawn.

After that it would be no true faith—it would be idle presumption—for us, who are habitually suitors and do not often rise to the level of servants, to imagine that we shall have any assurance which is not an illusion—or correct only by accident—about the event of our prayers. Our struggle is, isn't it?—to achieve and retain faith on a lower level. To believe that, whether He can grant them or not, God will listen to our prayers, will take them into account. Even to go on believing that there is a Listener at all. For as the situation grows more and more desperate, the grisly fears intrude. Are we only talking to ourselves in an empty universe? The silence is often so emphatic. And we have prayed so much already.

HOW DO WE PRAY
WHILE GRIEVING?

I NEED CHRIST, not something that resembles Him. I want H., not something that is like her. A really good photograph might become in the end a snare, a horror, and an obstacle.

Images, I must suppose, have their use or they would not have been so popular. (It makes little difference whether they are pictures and statues outside the mind or imaginative constructions within it.) To me, however, their danger is more obvious. Images of the Holy easily become holy images—sacrosanct. My idea of God is not a divine idea. It has to be

---

A Grief Observed (from chapter 4).

shattered time after time. He shatters it Himself. He is the great iconoclast. Could we not almost say that this shattering is one of the marks of His presence? The Incarnation is the supreme example; it leaves all previous ideas of the Messiah in ruins. And most are 'offended' by the iconoclasm; and blessed are those who are not. But the same thing happens in our private prayers.

All reality is iconoclastic. The earthly beloved, even in this life, incessantly triumphs over your mere idea of her. And you want her to; you want her with all her resistances, all her faults, all her unexpectedness. That is, in her foursquare and independent reality. And this, not any image or memory, is what we are to love still, after she is dead.

But 'this' is not now imaginable. In that respect H. and all the dead are like God. In that respect loving her has become, in its measure, like loving Him. In both cases I must stretch out the arms and hands of love—its eyes cannot here be used—to the reality, through—across—all the changeful phantasmagoria of my thoughts, passions, and imaginings. I mustn't sit down content with the phantasmagoria itself and worship that for Him, or love that for her.

Not my idea of God, but God. Not my idea of H., but H. Yes, and also not my idea of my neighbour, but my neighbour. For don't we often make this mistake as regards people who are still alive—who are with us in the same room? Talking and acting not to the man himself but to the picture—almost the *précis*—we've made of him in our own minds? And he has to depart from it pretty widely before we even notice the fact. In real life—that's one way it differs from novels—

I suppose the normal next step, after self-examination, repentance and restitution, is to make your Communion; and then to continue as well as you can, praying as well as you can... and fulfilling your daily duties as well as you can.

—*COLLECTED LETTERS*, JANUARY 4, 1941

his words and acts are, if we observe closely, hardly ever quite 'in character', that is, in what we call his character. There's always a card in his hand we didn't know about.

My reason for assuming that I do this to other people is the fact that so often I find them obviously doing it to me. We all think we've got one another taped.

And all this time I may, once more, be building with cards. And if I am He will once more knock the building flat. He will knock it down as often as proves necessary. Unless I have to be finally given up as hopeless, and left building pasteboard palaces in Hell forever; 'free among the dead.'

Am I, for instance, just sidling back to God because I know that if there's any road to H., it runs through Him? But then of course I know perfectly well that He can't be used as a road. If you're approaching Him not as the goal but as a road, not as the end but as a means, you're not really approaching Him at all.

That's what was really wrong with all those popular pictures of happy reunions 'on the further shore'; not the simple-minded and very earthly images, but the fact that they make an End of what we can get only as a by-product of the true End.

Lord, are these your real terms? Can I meet H. again only if I learn to love you so much that I don't care whether I meet her or not? Consider, Lord, how it looks to us. What would anyone think of me if I said to the boys, 'No toffee now. But when you've grown up and don't really want toffee you shall have as much of it as you choose'?

If I knew that to be eternally divided from H. and eternally forgotten by her would add a greater joy and splendour to her being, of course I'd say, 'Fire ahead.' Just as if, on earth, I could have cured her cancer by never seeing her again, I'd have arranged never to see her again. I'd have had to. Any decent person would. But that's quite different. That's not the situation I'm in.

When I lay these questions before God I get no answer. But a rather special sort of 'No answer.' It is not the locked door. It is more like a silent, certainly not uncompassionate, gaze. As though He shook His head not in refusal but waiving the question. Like, 'Peace, child; you don't understand.'

CAN WE PRAY TO AVOID SUFFERING IF IT IS GOOD FOR OUR SOUL?

THERE IS A paradox about tribulation in Christianity. Blessed are the poor, but by 'judgement' (i.e., social justice) and alms we are to remove poverty wherever possible. Blessed are we when persecuted, but we may avoid persecution by flying from city to city, and may pray to be spared it, as Our Lord prayed in Gethsemane. But if suffering is good, ought it not to be pursued rather than avoided? I answer that suffering is not good in itself. What is good in any painful

---

The Problem of Pain (from chapter 7, "Human Pain, Continued").

experience is, for the sufferer, his submission to the will of God, and, for the spectators, the compassion aroused and the acts of mercy to which it leads. In the fallen and partially redeemed universe we may distinguish (1) the simple good descending from God, (2) the simple evil produced by rebellious creatures, and (3) the exploitation of that evil by God for His redemptive purpose, which produces (4) the complex good to which accepted suffering and repented sin contribute. Now the fact that God can make complex good out of simple evil does not excuse—though by mercy it may save—those who do the simple evil. And this distinction is central. Offences must come, but woe to those by whom they come; sins *do* cause grace to abound, but we must not make that an excuse for continuing to sin. The crucifixion itself is the best, as well as the worst, of all historical events, but the role of Judas remains simply evil. We may apply this first to the problem of other people's suffering. A merciful man aims at his neighbour's good and so does 'God's will', consciously co-operating with 'the

❧

As to whether God ever wills suffering, I think [your priest] is confused. We must distinguish in God, and even in ourselves, absolute will from relative will. No one absolutely wills to have a tooth out, but many will to have a tooth out *rather than* to go on with toothache. Surely in the same way God never absolutely wills the least suffering for any creature, but may will it *rather than* some alternative: e.g., He willed the crucifixion rather than that Man shd. go unredeemed (and so it was *not*, in all senses, His will that the cup shd. pass from His Son).

—*COLLECTED LETTERS*, NOVEMBER 28, 1953, TO MARY VAN DEUSEN

simple good'. A cruel man oppresses his neighbour, and so does simple evil. But in doing such evil, he is used by God, without his own knowledge or consent, to produce the complex good—so that the first man serves God as a son, and the second as a tool. For you will certainly carry out God's purpose, however you act, but it makes a difference to you whether you serve like Judas or like John. The whole system is, so to speak, calculated for the clash between good men and bad men, and the good fruits of fortitude, patience, pity and forgiveness for which the cruel man is permitted to be cruel, presuppose that the good man ordinarily continues to seek simple good. I say 'ordinarily' because a man is sometimes entitled to hurt (or even, in my opinion, to kill) his fellow, but only where the necessity is urgent and the good to be attained obvious, and usually (though not always) when he who inflicts the pain has a definite authority to do so—a parent's authority derived from nature, a magistrate's or soldier's derived from civil society, or a surgeon's derived, most often, from the patient. To turn this into a general charter for afflicting humanity 'because affliction is good for them' (as Marlowe's lunatic Tamberlaine boasted himself the 'scourge of God') is not indeed to break the Divine scheme but to volunteer for the post of Satan within that scheme. If you do his work, you must be prepared for his wages.

The problem about avoiding our own pain admits a similar solution. Some ascetics have used self-torture. As a layman, I offer no opinion on the prudence of such a regimen; but I insist that, whatever its merits, self-torture is quite a different thing from tribulation sent by God. Everyone knows that fasting is a different experience from missing your dinner by accident or through poverty. Fasting asserts the will against the appetite—the reward being self-mastery and the danger pride: involuntary hunger subjects appetite and will together to the Divine will, furnishing an occasion for submission and exposing us to the danger of rebellion. But the redemptive effect of suffering lies chiefly in its tendency to reduce the rebel will. Ascetic practices, which in themselves strengthen the will, are only useful in so far as they enable the will to put its own house (the passions) in order, as a preparation for offering the whole man to God. They are necessary as a means; as an end, they would be abominable, for in substituting will for appetite and there stopping, they would merely exchange the animal self for the diabolical self. It was, therefore, truly said that 'only God can mortify'. Tribulation does its work in a world where human beings are ordinarily seeking, by lawful means, to avoid their own natural evil and to attain their natural good, and presupposes such a world. In order to submit the will to God, we must have a will and that will must have objects. Christian renunciation does not mean stoic 'Apathy', but a readiness to prefer God to inferior ends which are in themselves lawful. Hence the Perfect Man brought to Gethsemane a will, and a strong will, to escape suffering and death if such escape were compatible with the

The consoling thing is that while Christendom is divided about the rationality, and even the lawfulness, of praying *to* the saints, we are all agreed about praying *with* them. "With angels and archangels and all the company of heaven."

—*LETTERS TO MALCOLM*

Father's will, combined with a perfect readiness for obedience if it were not. Some of the saints recommend a 'total renunciation' at the very threshold of our discipleship; but I think this can mean only a total readiness for every particular renunciation that may be demanded, for it would not be possible to live from moment to moment willing nothing but submission to God as such. What would be the *material* for the submission? It would seem self-contradictory to say 'What I will is to subject what I will to God's will,' for the second *what* has no content. Doubtless we all spend too much care in the avoidance of our own pain: but a duly subordinated intention to avoid it, using lawful means, is in accordance with 'nature'— that is, with the whole working system of creaturely life for which the redemptive work of tribulation is calculated.

It would be quite false, therefore, to suppose that the Christian view of suffering is incompatible with the strongest emphasis on our duty to leave the world, even in a temporal sense, 'better' than we found it.

In the fullest parabolic picture which He gave of the Judgement, Our Lord seems to reduce all virtue to active beneficence: and though it would be misleading to take that one picture in isolation from the Gospel as a whole, it is sufficient to place beyond doubt the basic principles of the social ethics of Christianity.

HOW DO WE STAY HOPEFUL
WHEN GOD REPEATEDLY
SAYS NO TO OUR
REQUESTS FOR RELIEF?

ALL MAY YET be well. This is true. Meanwhile you have the waiting—waiting till the X-rays are developed and till the specialist has completed his observations. And while you wait, you still have to go on living—if only one could go underground, hibernate, sleep it out. And then (for me—I believe you are stronger) the horrible by-products of anxiety; the incessant, circular movement of the thoughts, even the Pagan temptation to keep watch for irrational omens.

Letters to Malcolm (from chapter 8).

And one prays; but mainly such prayers as are themselves a form of anguish.

Some people feel guilty about their anxieties and regard them as a defect of faith. I don't agree at all. They are afflictions, not sins. Like all afflictions, they are, if we can so take them, our share in the Passion of Christ. For the beginning of the Passion—the first move, so to speak—is in Gethsemane. In Gethsemane a very strange and significant thing seems to have happened.

It is clear from many of His sayings that Our Lord had long foreseen His death. He knew what conduct such as His, in a world such as we have made of this, must inevitably lead to. But it is clear that this knowledge must somehow have been withdrawn from Him before He prayed in Gethsemane. He could not, with whatever reservation about the Father's will, have prayed that the cup might pass and simultaneously known that it would not. That is both a logical and a psychological impossibility. You see what this involves? Lest any trial incident to humanity should be lacking, the torments of hope—of suspense, anxiety—were at the last moment loosed upon Him—the supposed possibility that, after all, He might, He just conceivably might, be spared the supreme horror. There was precedent. Isaac had been spared: he too at the last moment, he also against all apparent probability. It was not quite impossible . . . and doubtless He had seen other men crucified . . . a sight very unlike most of our religious pictures and images.

But for this last (and erroneous) hope against hope, and the consequent tumult of the soul, the sweat of blood, perhaps He would not have been very Man. To live in a fully predictable world is not to be a man.

At the end, I know, we are told that an angel appeared "comforting" him. But neither *comforting* in Sixteenth Century English nor ἐννισχύων in Greek means "consoling". "Strengthening" is more the word. May not the strengthening have consisted in the renewed certainty—cold comfort this—that the thing must be endured and therefore could be?

We all try to accept with some sort of submission our afflictions when they actually arrive. But the prayer in Gethsemane shows that the preceding anxiety is equally God's will and equally part of our human destiny. The perfect Man experienced it. And the servant is not greater than the master. We are Christians, not Stoics.

Does not every movement in the Passion write large some common element in the sufferings of our race? First, the prayer of anguish; not granted. Then He turns to His friends. They are asleep—as ours, or we, are so often, or busy, or away, or preoccupied. Then He faces the Church; the very Church that He brought into existence. It condemns Him. This is also characteristic. In every Church, in every institution, there is something which sooner or later works against the very purpose for which it came into existence. But there seems to be another chance. There is the State; in this case, the Roman state. Its pretensions are far lower than those of the Jewish church, but for that very reason it may be free from local fanaticisms.

Arise my body, my small body, we have striven
Enough, and He is merciful; we are forgiven.
Arise small body, puppet-like and pale, and go,
White as the bed-clothes into bed, and cold as
    snow,
Undress with small, cold fingers and put out the
    light,
And be alone, hush'd mortal, in the sacred night,
—A meadow whipt flat with the rain, a cup
Emptied and clean, a garment washed and
    folded up,
Faded in colour, thinned almost to raggedness
By dirt and by the washing of that dirtiness.
Be not too quickly warm again. Lie cold;
    consent
To weariness' and pardon's watery element.
Drink up the bitter water, breathe the chilly
    death;
Soon enough comes the riot of our blood and
    breath.

—"AFTER PRAYERS, LIE COLD," *POEMS*

It claims to be just, on a rough, worldly level. Yes, but only so far as is consistent with political expediency and *raison d'état*. One becomes a counter in a complicated game. But even now all is not lost. There is still an appeal to the People—the poor and simple whom He had blessed, whom He had healed and fed and taught, to whom He himself belongs. But they have become over-night (it is nothing unusual) a murderous rabble shouting for His blood. There is, then, nothing left but God. And to God, God's last words are, "Why hast thou forsaken me?"

You see how characteristic, how representative, it all is. The human situation writ large. These are among the things it means to be a man. Every rope breaks when you seize it. Every door is slammed shut as you reach it. To be like the fox at the end of the run; the earths all staked.

As for the last dereliction of all, how can we either understand or endure it? Is it that God Himself cannot be Man unless God seems to vanish at His greatest need? And if so, why? I sometimes wonder if we have even begun to understand what is involved in the very concept of creation. If God will create, He will make something to be, and yet to be not Himself. To be created is, in some sense, to be ejected or separated. Can it be that the more perfect the creature is, the further this separation must at some point be pushed? It is saints, not common people, who experience the "dark night". It is men and angels, not beasts, who rebel. Inanimate matter sleeps in the bosom of the Father. The "hiddenness" of God perhaps presses most painfully on those who are in another way nearest to Him, and therefore God Himself, made man, will of all men be by God most forsaken? One of the Seventeenth Century divines says: "By pretending to be visible God could only deceive the world." Perhaps He does pretend just a little to simple souls who need a full measure of "sensible consolation". Not deceiving them, but tempering the wind to the shorn lamb. Of course I'm not saying like Niebühr that evil is inherent in finitude. That would identify the creation with the fall and make God the author of evil. But perhaps there is an anguish, an alienation, a crucifixion involved in the creative act. Yet He who alone can judge judges the far-off consummation to be worth it.

I am, you see, a Job's comforter. Far from lightening the dark valley where you now find yourself, I blacken it. And you know why. Your darkness has brought back my own. But on second thoughts I don't regret what I have written. I think it is only in a shared darkness that you and I can really meet at present; shared with one another and, what matters most, with our Master. We are not on an untrodden path. Rather, on the main-road.

Certainly we were talking too lightly and easily about these things a fortnight ago. We were playing with counters. One used to be told as a child: "Think what you're saying." Apparently we need also to be told: "Think what you're thinking." The stakes have to be raised before we take the game quite seriously. I know this is the opposite of what is often said about the necessity of keeping all emotion out of our intellectual processes—"You can't think straight unless you are cool [unexcited]." But then neither can you think deep if you are. I suppose one must try every problem in both states. You remember that the ancient Persians debated everything twice: once when they were drunk and once when they were sober.

I know one of you will let me have news as soon as there is any.